Pass Tr

GESE

Contents

Contents

Phonology	Exam expert Topic (T) & Conversation (C)	Exam expert Interactive (I) & Listening (L)
Stress in two-syllable words	Selecting a topic for grade 9 (T)	Introduction to the phase (I)
Topic and subject-area vocabulary	Researching subject areas (C)	Understanding the prompt (I)
Speaking with enthusiasm	Mind maps & note taking (T)	Controlling the Interactive Phase (I)
Intonation to convey attitude	Responding to the examiner (C)	Maintaining & developing the discourse (I)
Stress in sentences	Anticipating examiner questions (T)	Using functions of the grade (I)
Intonation of question tags	Engaging the examiner in the topic (T)	Exam practice (I)
Using pause and intonation to give clarity	Grade 10 subject areas (C)	Introduction & exam practice (L)
Stress in longer words	Formal topic presentation & discussion (T)	What the candidate needs to do (I)
–	Preparing a formal presentation (T)	Identifying context & participants (L)
Weak forms	Responding to the examiner (T)	Anticipating what happens next (L)
Intonation of intensifiers & modifiers	Sharing responsibility (C)	Using functions of the grade (I)
–	Presentation & discussion (T) Exam practice (C)	Exam practice (I) Exam practice (L)

Exam overview

TRINITY GRADED EXAMINATIONS IN SPOKEN ENGLISH (GESE), GRADES 9 AND 10

GESE Grade 9 (CEFR B2.3)

Time: 15 minutes

Format and procedure

At the beginning of the exam you and the examiner will exchange greetings and have a moment to relax before starting the Topic phase.

1 Discussion of a **topic prepared by the candidate** (up to 5 minutes)

   You will lead a discussion on your prepared topic with the examiner. You will be expected to communicate facts, ideas, opinions and attitudes in a structured way. You should be able to interact with the examiner and respond to questions as well as handle interruptions and clarify and emphasise points where necessary.

2 **Interactive task** (up to 4 minutes)

   After the examiner has read out the prompt, you are responsible for starting and maintaining the conversation by asking for information and developing the discussion. You will take turns with the examiner using the appropriate language functions of the grade to encourage comment and opinion from the examiner..

3 **Conversation on two subject areas** selected by the examiner (up to 5 minutes)

   You will answer questions about two subject areas selected by the examiner from the list for Grade 9. You will share responsibility for developing and maintaining the conversation and respond to the examiner's comments. In the case of a breakdown in communication, you may need to paraphrase or rephrase.

At the end of the conversation phase you will say goodbye and leave the examination room.

Grade 9 exam syllabus:

Grammar
- Verbs followed by gerund and/or infinitive
- More complex forms of the passive with modals
- *should/must/might/could* + present perfect tense
- Correct verb patterns after wish and hope
- Mixed conditionals

Subject areas for Conversation phase
- Dreams & nightmares
- Crime & punishment
- Technology
- Habits & obsessions
- Global environmental issues
- Design

Functions
- Expressing abstract ideas
- Expressing regrets, wishes and hopes
- Expressing assumptions
- Paraphrasing
- Evaluating options
- Hypothesising
- Evaluating past actions or course of events

Phonology
- Correct pronunciation of words relevant to the vocabulary for this grade
- Rising and falling intonation for keeping, giving up and offering turns
- Stress and rhythm to highlight and emphasise main points and ideas
- Intonation and pitch to convey attitude

GESE Grade 10 (CEFR C1.1)

Time: 25 minutes

Format and procedure

1 **Topic presentation** (up to 5 minutes)

You will give the examiner a handout before starting a formal discursive presentation which you have prepared. It should be organised in a structured way with an introduction, the development of points (giving examples and reasons) and finally a conclusion. Then you will ask the examiner to comment or ask questions.

2 **Topic discussion** (up to 5 minutes)

You will initiate the discussion about your presentation and share responsibility with the examiner for its development. You will respond to the examiner's questions and be prepared to defend your point of view or develop the argument further.

3 **Interactive task** (up to 5 minutes)

After the examiner has read out the prompt, you are responsible for the direction and maintenance of the interaction. You will take turns with the examiner by commenting and asking questions so that interaction develops naturally.

4 **Listening phase** (up to 3 minutes)

The examiner will read out three short listening texts. In the first two you will tell the examiner in just a few words how you think the passage finishes. In the third text you will answer a question about the context and the people involved.

5 **Conversation on two subject areas** selected by the examiner (up to 6 minutes)

The examiner will ask you questions about two subject areas from either List A or List B. You will share responsibility with the examiner for the maintenance and direction of the conversation and will participate naturally without hesitation.

Grade 10 exam syllabus:

Language and grammar
- Vocabulary specific to the topic and subject areas
- A range of idiomatic expressions and colloquialisms
- Modifying words, e.g. *basically*, *quite*, *certainly*
- Intensifiers, e.g. *absolutely*, *completely*, *totally*
- Tentative expressions, e.g. *I may be wrong but...* *Don't you think it might be...*
- Signposting words, e.g. *firstly*, *finally*
- A broad range of complex structures to express thoughts clearly
- A high degree of grammatical accuracy, although minor errors may occur when attempting to use a combination of structures across sentence boundaries

Functions
- Developing an argument
- Defending a point of view
- Expressing beliefs
- Expressing opinions tentatively
- Summarising information, ideas and arguments
- Deducing

Subject areas for Conversation phase

List A
Roles in the family
Communication
The school curriculum
Youth behaviour
Use of the Internet
Designer goods

List B
International events
Equal opportunities
Social issues
The future of the planet
Scientific development
Stress management

Phonology
- The correct pronunciation of words relevant to the vocabulary at this grade
- Sounds with minimal interference from the first language
- A range of stress and intonation patterns, pitch and volume to: engage and maintain the examiner's interest; signal the provision of new information; indicate discourse structure.

Technology

B

ARE YOU TECHY?

1 You have your mobile phone switched on
   A all the time.   **B** when you want to make a call.
   C when you are alone.

2 You use a computer
   A 1-2 hours a day.   **B** 6 hours or more a day.   **C** rarely.

3 When you get a new high-tech gadget you
   A enjoy experimenting and working out how to use it.
   B ask someone to help you.
   C put it away in a drawer until you are in the mood.

4 When you receive an email you
   A reply after a few days.   **B** ask someone to open it for you.
   C reply immediately.

5 When you need to drive somewhere you
   A look up the route on the internet.   **B** use sat nav.
   C look at a map.

6 To send a quick message you
   A send a text.   **B** use the phone.   **C** send an email.

7 To find out about new music you
   A go to a music shop.
   B download from the Internet onto your MP3 player.
   C listen to your digital radio.

8 When you take photographs you use your
   A old camera and take it to a shop to get it developed.
   B digital camera and get a friend to print off the photos.
   C digital camera and print the photos on your computer.

D

C

E

F

Vocabulary

1a Look at the pictures of recent technological inventions on the previous page (A-F) and match them to the list (1-6) below.

1. ☐ Sat Nav (Satellite navigation)
2. ☐ touch-screen phone
3. ☐ laptop
4. ☐ digital camera
5. ☐ USB flash drive
6. ☐ MP3 player

b Talk to your partner and decide, (a) how important these inventions are in your lives, and (b) what their advantages and disadvantages are.

2a Complete the questionnaire on page 6 to find out how techy you are.

b Now compare your answers with a partner and then decide which of you is the most comfortable with new technology. Then check your scores at the back of the book on page 93.

Listening

3a 🔊 Listen to the five people and note down what kind of technology or which gadget has changed each person's life.

1. John ....
2. Maria ....
3. Kieran ....
4. Dani ....
5. Mike ....

b 🔊 Listen again and note down how technology has changed their lives.

E.g. John receives hundreds of emails and loves it.

c Now in pairs talk about your favourite technological gadget and give reasons. Take notes and tell the rest of the class.

Reading

4a Read the information below and decide what Aboutyou.com is.

b What impressions do you get of Jack? Tell another student what kind of things you would put on your homepage.

Aboutyou.com   Search [🔍]   Home   Profile   Find friends   Account ▼

About Me:
Name: Jack Cox
Birthday: 11 November 1988
City: Oxford
Loves: reggae, travelling in Asia and politics

Friends:
387

Holly   Emma   Sam   Adam

Jack says:

April 10. Back in Oxford. Love it!
April 11. Exam timetable out. Finish June 7.

Jack's friends' say:

Love your hat. Elise x
Got my air ticket to India for August 10.
Wanna come? Adam

Aboutyou.com

About you, about me.

These days I hardly ever go out to meet old friends or even make new ones. Rarely do I venture into a bar or club to socialise or listen to the latest band in town. You'll usually find me in my tiny university room peering at a laptop screen with my fingers moving rapidly across the keyboard.

Sad or what? That's doubtless what you all might think. No friends... never goes out. The latter is probably true but no friends, certainly not. Would you believe I've got 387 now. 387 I hear you say. Impossible! Well, OK it's not quite the same as meeting people face to face but it doesn't mean to say it's not valuable. It's such a brilliant idea, really, and means I can keep in touch with all my friends both at home, here at uni and of course all those people I met while travelling in Asia last year.

Another great advantage of Aboutyou is the opportunity to make new friends.

Once you have set up your own homepage giving information about yourself such as interests and lifestyle, you'll quickly identify like-minded people and build many new online relationships. A word of warning – only accept friends you already know or are sure you can trust. You can turn down anybody you're suspicious about. I've never had any problems but I know some people who have.

So how exactly do you communicate? Well, if you'd like your life to remain private then it's probably best to send personal messages that nobody else can read. However, most of us thoroughly enjoy telling everyone on Aboutyou every trivial detail of our lives and then your friends move in to comment. You can also post photos of holidays and nights out.

So, as you can see, Aboutyou is a fun way of socialising. You may be alone with your computer but in fact you're never alone. Could the future be social death without Aboutyou?

5a Read the text quickly and discuss in pairs what else you now know about Jack.

b Now read the text again and discuss in pairs the questions below.

1 What is the prime function of Aboutyou?

2 What are the differences between an Aboutyou friendship and a face-to-face one?

3 What risks do you think there might be in using Aboutyou?

4 What in your view is the reason for the popularity of such social networking sites, especially among young people?

5 What does Jack mean when he says it could be social death without Aboutyou?

Grammar focus

Grammar review

6a Look at the structures (A-J) and match them to the correct sentence (1-10).

A *Going to* (future)　**F** Third conditional
B Present perfect　**G** Passive
C Present perfect continuous　**H** Past perfect
D *Will* (future)　**I** Reported speech
E Second conditional　**J** Modal verbs

1 ☐ I had been there many times before.

2 ☐ You really should do more work!

3 ☐ Thousands of computers are produced in China every year.

4 ☐ My grandmother has lived in a village all her life.

5 ☐ The director said the film was a great success.

6 ☐ If I joined Aboutyou.com, I would make loads of friends.

7 ☐ I think he'll be a brilliant politician.

8 ☐ We've been studying English for 5 years, haven't we?

9 ☐ My brother is going to get married next year.

10 ☐ If he hadn't worked so hard, he wouldn't have got into university last year.

b Complete the following sentences using the correct form of the verb in brackets.

1 My father .... in a big factory since 1972. (work)

2 If he .... at home that night, he wouldn't have had that terrible accident. (stay)

3 Thousands of emails .... every minute of the day. (send)

4 If I were rich, I .... money to charity. (give)

5 .... she always .... early? (get up)

6 I really think he .... rich and famous in the future. (be)

c In pairs answer the following questions.

1 How long have you been learning English?

2 If you were the leader of your country, what changes would you make?

3 What products are made in your region?

4 What did your family say to you before you left home this morning?

5 What do you think you will do in the future?

Phonology

■ Stress in two-syllable words

Word stress in English is variable. In a two-syllable word the stress might fall on the first or second syllable. Unfortunately, if you put the stress on the wrong part of the word it can sound completely different and make it unintelligible to a native speaker. Fortunately, in most two-syllable words the stress is on the first syllable.

7a 🔊 Listen to the following words and repeat.

1 'laptop

2 'email

3 'mobile

4 'photo

5 'gadget

6 'homepage

7 'website

8 'access

GRADE 9

b In pairs try saying the word with the WRONG stress (i.e. on the second syllable) and see how different it sounds.

c 🔊 04 Of course there are some exceptions to this rule! Listen to the following and repeat.

1 a'sleep   3 a'lone   5 con'trol
2 mis'take   4 ma'chine

d Most two-syllable verbs have stress on the second syllable.

E.g. *e'scape   for'get   en'joy*

🔊 05 Listen to the 5 groups of two-syllable words below. Circle the word with a different stress pattern from the others.

1 remove   regret   reason
2 shopping   shovel   shampoo
3 careful   complete   crazy
4 agree   answer   alone
5 middle   mistake   mimic

Function focus

▪ Evaluating options

Imagine that you would like to buy a new mobile phone and have been looking at the various options available. You are now discussing with a friend which one to buy. You might say:

'If I buy a Kandy BT4, it will cost a lot of money. It might be better to buy a cheaper model.'

'It would be great to have a touch screen phone. Perhaps I'll get a Moon 8500.'

'I should get an Easy 1200. It doesn't cost very much and I only need it to phone and text. But look how cool the Gull 6600 is…'

8 Look at the features and prices of these mobile phones and in pairs discuss the best option for each of you. Report back to the rest of the class which ones you have chosen and why.

	Gull 6600	**Kandy BT4**	**Moon 8500**	**Easy 1200**
Touchscreen	No	Yes	Yes	No
Wi-Fi	No	Yes	No	No
Camera	Yes	Yes	Yes	No
Video Recording	No	No	Yes	No
Music player	Yes	Yes	Yes	No
Headphones	Yes	Yes	Yes	No
FM Radio	Yes	No	No	No
Colour	Pink or black	Black	White or orange	Black
Price	£300	£600	£270	£40

Topic phase

Selecting a topic for Grade 9

9a Work with a partner and make a list of as many topics as you can think of. Then on your own pick out three favourites.

1 ....

2 ....

3 ....

b In pairs ask each other the questions below. If all these statements are correct, it is probably a good topic for you.

1 ☐ It isn't on the list of subject areas for the conversation.

2 ☐ The topic would stimulate discussion with the examiner.

3 ☐ It would be possible to use the language required for the grade.

4 ☐ It isn't a topic that would be more suitable for a lower grade.

c 06 🔊 Now listen to four students talking about their choice of topic and decide if they are suitable (Y) or not (N).

1 ☐ Rosa   3 ☐ Tham

2 ☐ Stefano   4 ☐ Florian

Interactive phase

Introduction to the phase

The Interactive phase is different to the other parts of the exam. This is what the examiner says to you:

For the next part, I'll tell you something. Then you have to ask me questions to find out more information. You need to keep the conversation going. After about 4 minutes, I'll end the conversation. Are you ready?

Then listen carefully to the prompt:

When I was <u>young</u> I did something I am very <u>ashamed</u> of – now I simply <u>can't forget</u> about it.

These underlined words tell you:

- It happened a long time ago – your questions will be in the past tense.
- The examiner feels very bad about it – you might give him or her advice.

10a Look at the interactive prompts below and underline the key words and discuss why they are important.

> ¹ I really don't know what to do in the future. I had a great idea the other day, but now I'm not so sure.

> ² Someone stole my friend's computer last week. She thinks she knows who did it, but is not absolutely sure.

b Now for each prompt, think of the first question you might ask the examiner.

E.g. When I was young I did something I am very ashamed of...

Really! What exactly did you do?

c Turn to page 93 and do the quiz.

Examiner: Which of these phones would you like to buy?
Candidate: Well, **it would be great** to have a touch screen phone but **it might be better** to buy a cheaper model.

UNIT 2

Crime & punishment

Vocabulary

1a In pairs look at the pictures above and talk about what crimes they represent.

b Now use some of the words below to label the pictures.

> arson   bribery   smoking in public places
> cybercrime   robbery   pickpocketing   burglary
> drug trafficking   dumping rubbish   pollution
> drink driving   shoplifting

Do you know the meaning of all these words? Look them up in a dictionary or ask your teacher. Which ones do you think are crimes?

c Now order this list from 1-12 with 1 the most serious and 12 the least serious.

d Discuss in pairs if any of the crimes are particularly common in your town or country. Then add to the list any other crimes that are common in your area.

Reading

2a Discuss in groups what you think cybercrime is.

b Read through the text and find out:

1   what the main cybercrimes mentioned here are.

2   what steps you should take to protect yourself.

c Complete the following sentences using the words underlined in the text.

1 When you want to use an online account you will have to enter your ....

2 Stealing somebody's personal information in order to access their bank account is called ....

3 .... is somebody who is obsessed with computers.

4 An .... behaves as dishonestly as is necessary in order to get what he wants.

5 Breaking into computer networks is known as ....

6 You will have to .... if you want to stop anybody accessing it.

7 A .... is an illegal way of making money.

8 If you have had a life of crime, you are probably a ....

d Discuss in pairs if you would be prepared to disclose sensitive information online to buy things.

CYBERCRIME
The crime of the century!

Katy Poon
Address: Flat 2, 42 West Street, Manchester
Email katy@friend.com
Bank: Asia International
Bank Code: 01423000
Account Number: 22445562

Cybercrime is the fastest growing crime in the 21st century and covers a huge range of illegal activities including <u>hacking</u> into computer networks and stealing information.

Criminals have been quick to spot its potential realising that they can make much more money than in other riskier and often more violent areas of crime. It's a job that does not require sophisticated technical skills and appeals both to the <u>hardened criminal</u> and the inexperienced <u>computer geek</u>. They can easily work from home only abandoning their computer to collect their cash. So how exactly is this cash generated? A <u>financial scam</u> involves setting up a bogus company on the Internet in order to convince victims that they are a reputable site It may sell attractive products at bargain prices but the unsuspecting online buyer will have to provide their credit card details to complete the purchase. They will then find, to their horror, that the site disappears and they have no way of retrieving either their bank details or their money. Considering how common this type of crime is, it is astonishing that the general public continue to be conned in this way. If they only realised what they were doing they would surely not get involved.

Another form of cybercrime is <u>identity theft</u>. This does not necessarily involve hacking at all. Criminals can surf the web or other databases for personal information such as dates of birth, insurance numbers and addresses. They may even access this information by searching through people's rubbish bins if they are prepared to get their hands dirty. These details are then used to apply for credit cards and the cyber criminal can go on a global spending spree.

So what can be done to protect you and me from the <u>unscrupulous cyber criminal</u>? Be cautious about what information you share online and keep your security software up to date. Create a difficult to guess <u>password</u> for online accounts and vary them so if one of your accounts is compromised you won't have to worry about the others. If you are suspicious about a website, do not attempt to use it and always be cautious about opening emails from unknown sources. If, despite all this, you become a victim, you should disconnect from the Internet, <u>freeze your bank account</u> immediately and inform the police.

GRADE 9

3a Look at the headlines about Bernard Madoff and discuss what they reveal about him.

> **Madoff millions vanish into thin air**

> *Madoff with your money!*

> **Madoff dubbed King Con**

> Madoff caged for 150 years today

b Read the article and discuss whether a 150-year prison sentence is the most appropriate punishment for a man like this.

29th June 2009

Bernard Madoff was jailed for 150 years today after committing the biggest scam in history.

A respected Wall Street financier, he was able to convince businessmen and tiny charities alike that he was offering a safe investment. There was little about him to raise suspicions and much to inspire trust. He was rich and successful, and a New York socialite.

To everyone's horror, he turned out to be a professional conman and managed to defraud investors of $50 billion. His scheme only lasted as long as there was enough new investment to pay investors who wanted to withdraw money and the operation fell apart when he didn't have it.

Now millions of people have been left destitute and deprived of the comfortable retirement they were looking forward to.

Listening

4a 🎧 Being in prison is, of course, not supposed to be an enjoyable experience, but it can provide some opportunities for inmates. Listen to Jack Dunwoody talking about an interesting new scheme. Was it successful?

b 🎧 Listen again and then in pairs discuss what these words mean. You can use your dictionary or ask your teacher.

> illiterate stimulating innovative enhance
> compulsory intimidate inmate

c 🎧 Listen once more and decide if these statements are true (T), false (F) or don't know (DK).

1 ☐ Many inmates have learning difficulties.
2 ☐ The new classes were rather boring.
3 ☐ Offenders had to attend classes.
4 ☐ They introduced foreign language classes.
5 ☐ One of the students won first prize in a competition.
6 ☐ The men feel a lot more positive about the future.

Vocabulary

■ **Easily-confused words:** *rob, steal, and burgle.*

> A **robber** or **thief robs** things, especially money, from a place (e.g. a bank) or a person.
> A **robber** or **thief steals** things from a place or person.
> A **burglar burgles** a house by forcing a way in and stealing from it. This is a **bulgary**.

5 Now put in the right form of *rob, steal* or *burgle* in the sentences below.

1 Last night an armed gang .... the post office. They .... €10,000.
2 My wallet .... on the train yesterday.
3 My flat .... and everything has gone.
4 The .... stole a great deal of money from the supermarket.
5 My neighbours were burgled last night. The police haven't caught the .... yet.

Grammar focus

Mixed conditionals

We often use conditionals to express hypothetical situations in the present and past.

This is EITHER a second conditional present time:
If I **had** a computer, I **would shop** online (but I don't have a computer so I don't shop online).

OR a third conditional past conditional.
If I **hadn't used** my credit card to shop online, they **wouldn't have got** my bank details (but I did and they got my bank details).

Sometimes we want to imagine past events with results in the present. These sentences are called mixed conditionals.

E.g. If Bernard Madoff **hadn't stolen** all that money, he **would be** a free man today.
= He stole the money (past) and he isn't a free man now (present).

6a Complete sentences 1-4 with clauses A-D.

1 ☐ She would be rich now
2 ☐ He wouldn't have been sent to prison
3 ☐ If he hadn't committed fraud,
4 ☐ They would be here by now

A if they had caught the flight.
B he would still live in his new York apartment.
C if he were innocent.
D if she had married him.

b Now complete the following sentences with a mixed conditional.

1 If I had studied harder, I ....
2 If he ...., he would be rich now.
3 If John hadn't driven so fast, ...
4 I would be hungry now if I .... not ....
5 If she ...., she wouldn't be in prison now.

c Now complete the following sentences with the correct form of the conditional. Choose either a second, third or mixed conditional.

1 If he had taken his phone, ...
2 I wouldn't hesitate if ....
3 If she hadn't told him about John, ...
4 They would have enjoyed the holiday more if ....
5 I would be totally happy if ....
6 If I were you, ...
7 They wouldn't be here now if ....
8 If he asked me again, ...

GRADE 9

Function focus

Hypothesising

We often hypothesise to give a possible explanation for an event, to discuss or imagine various possibilities. Sometimes we are looking back into the past or we may be considering current or future situations. To do this we may use conditionals or modals. Let's think about inmates in prison and what they might say about their life past and present.

E.g. I could live on a Caribbean island if I weren't stuck in here.
If I hadn't got involved in cybercrime, I might have had a good job in computer technology.

7a Now in pairs imagine how life could have been different for you.

'I could have had a more relaxed life if I'd chosen to live in the country.'

b Now in pairs hypothesise about future changes in your country and how your lives might change as a result. Complete the mind map and make sentences.

E.g. If cars were banned, we might all get more exercise.

The construction of new cities might mean more employment opportunities for the young.

Phonology

Topic and subject-area vocabulary

You may choose to use some long and complicated words in the exam and it is very important that you know how to pronounce them. In English the syllables in a word do not have equal stress and if you put the stress on the wrong part of the word, you may not be understood by a native speaker. For the Trinity exam you can prepare yourself well by checking with your teacher or the dictionary. Most dictionaries use /'/ to show where the stress in a word is.

8a Look at the list of words from this unit and practise saying them in pairs.

1	cybercrime	6	inmate
2	potential	7	illiterate
3	unscrupulous	8	investment
4	identity	9	professional
5	appropriate	10	burgle

b 🔊 Now listen to the recording and add a /'/ to the part of the word that you think is stressed. Then check your answers with your teacher.

c Now practise saying the words again concentrating on getting the stress right.

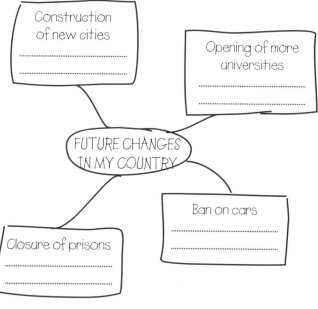

Construction of new cities
....
....

Opening of more universities
....
....

FUTURE CHANGES IN MY COUNTRY

Ban on cars
....
....

Closure of prisons
....
....

Conversation phase

Researching subject areas

9a Read the following statements about the conversation phase and decide if they are true (T) or false (F).

1. ☐ The examiner will ask you about 3 subject areas.
2. ☐ The conversation phase lasts up to 10 minutes.
3. ☐ It's the last phase of the exam.
4. ☐ You need to prepare vocabulary and ideas for 6 subject areas.
5. ☐ You should try and use the grammar and functions of the grade.
6. ☐ You don't need to comment or ask questions.

b Now prepare for the Crime & punishment subject area by completing the following table.

Vocabulary
cybercrime, shoplifting

Examiner's Questions
If you were a politician in your country, what would you do to reduce crime?
What new crimes have increased since the development of computer technology?

Your answers

Your questions
Would you be worried about identity theft if you shopped online?

Interactive phase

Understanding the prompt

It is very important that you understand every detail of the prompt. If you don't, then you might ask the examiner the wrong questions and not be able to resolve the situation.

10 Take turns in reading out the following prompts to each other and then discuss:

1. who the prompt is talking about – the examiner, a relative, a friend, etc;
2. what the situation is;
3. where the problem/difficulty lies;
4. what functions you might use.

> **A** My brother has just been offered a fantastic new job. The only problem is that it's in Australia.

> **B** I've just given my credit card details to a total stranger. Now I'm beginning to regret it.

> **C** My husband has just booked an expensive climbing holiday for us both in the Alps. I'm absolutely terrified and don't know how to tell him.

Trinity **TAKE** AWAY

Examiner: How do you think your life **could have been** different?
Candidate: I **could have got** a university degree if **I'd worked** harder.

Design

A

B

C

D

Vocabulary

1a Look at the pictures above. Are they good or bad designs? Discuss in pairs their aesthetic qualities and their functional value.

b Look at the building on the right and decide which of the following adjectives best describe it. Use a dictionary or ask your teacher if you don't understand any of the words.

> traditional   conventional   state-of-the-art
> radical   retro   outrageous
> stunning   innovative

c To what extent do you consider this building a work of art? Would you like to stay in a hotel like this? Why/why not?

Frank Gehry: Dream Builder

World-famous architect, Frank Gehry, was born in Canada in 1929 and became interested in design as a child when he used to create models out of wood for his grandmother. He moved to California in 1947, got a job as a truck driver and eventually graduated from the South California School of Architecture. He spent many years working in traditional architecture but began to [1] *develop a more radical approach* creating buildings with abstract forms and wild features. This was first exemplified in his own home in Santa Monica, which has an [2] *almost unfinished, chaotic appearance.*

Many of his designs were viewed as totally impracticable so he remained largely [3] *a 'paper architect'* until the design of the Guggenheim Museum in Bilbao won him [4] *international acclaim*. Since then he has received major commissions for iconic buildings around the world and has achieved [5] *'starchitect' status*. His critics argue that he is famous for the spectacle of his buildings rather than their real architectural value and that more attention should be given to [6] *harmonising them with* their natural surroundings. However, it cannot be denied that his eye-catching titanium clad landmarks are an important influence in modern architecture.

One of Frank Gehry's latest creations is the Hotel Marqués de Riscal in the Spanish wine-growing region of Rioja. Its swirling titanium ribbons are [7] *juxtaposed with* the nineteenth-century architecture of the original farmhouse and a backdrop of glorious rolling countryside. The [8] *locals understandably feel ambivalent* about it, but now many tourists are being drawn to a previously little-known area.

Gehry should have the last word on the matter, 'I wanted to create something festive and exciting because wine is about pleasure!'

Guggenheim Museum, Bilbao.

Reading

2a The hotel on page 18 was designed by Frank Gehry. Read the article quickly and discuss what is unusual about his work.

b Read the text again and explain what each of these phrases means in context.

1 develop a more radical approach...
2 almost unfinished, chaotic appearance
3 a 'paper architect'...
4 international acclaim
5 'starchitect' status
6 harmonising them with...
7 juxtaposed with...
8 locals... feel ambivalent...

c Think of buildings in your country or region. Are there any examples of iconic buildings such as the pyramids in Egypt or the Roman Colosseum? Are there any buildings that you have visited or would like to visit that are both eye-catching and functional?

GRADE 9

Grammar focus

Modals with the passive

We can use modals to express possibility, ability, obligation and recommendation. *Should, ought to, must, have to, can, would, might* and *will* are all modal verbs.

We can use these modals with the passive to change the focus of the sentence or to make it more formal. In this case the infinitive of the verb 'to be' follows the modal verb.
E.g. *More attention should be given to harmonising them (the buildings) with their surroundings.*

3a Match each sentence (1-6) to a sentence with a similar meaning (A-F).

1 ☐ That awful building should never have been given planning permission.

2 ☐ I have to go to university today.

3 ☐ That policy might be changed in the future.

4 ☐ She ought not to have eaten so much junk food.

5 ☐ We could go to that new restaurant tonight.

6 ☐ Look! This must be the right house.

A We have found what we are looking for.

B Why ever did they allow it to be built?

C There's a possibility it will be done differently.

D She ate far too many burgers.

E It's one of the places we are considering.

F It's the first day of my course.

b Look at the photos and in pairs or groups discuss the clothes. Give your opinion using the expressions below.

As far as I'm concerned...
I do think...
I have to say...
It's unbelievable! It's amazing!
It could be argued...
Would anyone wear that?
It cannot be denied...
It's a dress to die for, isn't it?

c Now using modal verbs make suggestions for changes to the clothes.

E.g. *I do think the dress should be a different colour.*
The suit ought to be redesigned.

'Art is a lie that makes us realize truth.'

Pablo Picasso

'Design is not just what it looks like. Design is how it works.'

Steve Jobs, Inventor and founder of Apple

Function focus

Expressing abstract ideas

4 Read the quotes and discuss the following in pairs.

1 What was Picasso saying about art?

2 What was Steve Jobs saying about design?

We use the abstract to talk about general ideas and concepts rather than the specific or personal. It tends to be more formal.

E.g. Pete is one of my best friends. (specific)

Friendship has great significance in people's lives. (abstract)

5a What abstract nouns can be formed from these adjectives?

0 happy *happiness* **3** true ....

1 lovely .... **4** peaceful ....

2 beautiful .... **5** friendly ....

b Now make sentences using the adjectives and abstract nouns in a).

E.g. Happiness is...

c Discuss these questions.

1 What do you think of architecture today?

2 Is crime a problem in all societies?

3 Is technology a vital part of our lives?

4 Is fashion design just a way of making money?

Listening

6a You are going to listen to a young fashion designer talking about her career. Before you start, think of five things she might talk about.

E.g. interest in fashion

b 🔊 Listen to the interview and answer the following questions.

1 Why is the journalist interviewing Victoria now?

2 How did she become a fashion designer?

3 What did she find hard?

4 What do we know about her collection?

Phonology

Speaking with enthusiasm

7a 🔊 Listen to the two speakers. Which speaker do you want to listen to more?

The first speaker's voice rises at the end. He also gives greater stress to the key words in the sentence, such as verbs and nouns.

b 🔊 Listen and underline the stressed words.

1 I'd like to speak about abstract ideas.

2 I would like to tell you about fashion design.

3 Actually, my topic is hip hop music.

4 I've chosen to talk about cultural differences in Europe.

c Now in pairs practise saying the sentences in b) in an enthusiastic way.

exam EXPERT

Topic phase

■ Mind maps & note taking

8 Read the statements below about the topic phase and decide if they are true (T) or false (F).

1. ☐ The topic phase lasts up to 5 minutes.
2. ☐ You should memorise your topic.
3. ☐ You don't need a topic form.
4. ☐ It is advisable to use notes or diagrams.
5. ☐ The topic should be chosen from the list of subject areas.
6. ☐ The examiner will ask you questions about your topic.
7. ☐ You should try and include the specific language of the grade.
8. ☐ You mustn't express any opinions.

9a Look at the mind map below for the topic 'My Cultural Exchange'. There are examples of areas to think about and relevant language. Now prepare your own mind map for the topic you chose in Unit 1.

b Based on the information on your mind map, prepare clear and simple notes that you can take into the exam room with you.

c In pairs role-play the Topic phase.

Candidate A: You are the examiner. Begin like this:

We'll start with the topic. What have you chosen to talk about?

Candidate B: You are the student. Talk about your topic and answer questions on it.

Then swap roles and repeat the task. When you have finished, discuss what you learnt from the role play.

E.g. *Did you have too much information?*
Could you answer all the questions?

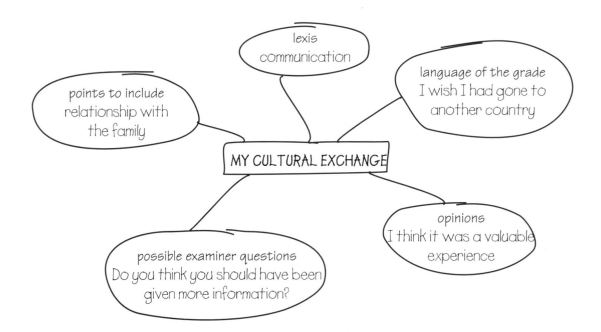

Interactive phase

■ **Controlling the Interactive phase**

During the Interactive phase you are responsible for controlling the interaction, so it's very important that you listen to the examiner, respond appropriately and ask the right questions.

10a Read the prompt and answer the questions.

> My brother has just been offered a fantastic new job with a firm of architects. The only problem is that it's in Australia.

  1 What are the two key facts?
  2 What is the first question you would ask?

b 🔊 **Listen to a candidate talking about the prompt and decide if the following comments are true (T), false (F) or don't know (DK).**

  1 ☐ The student focused on the positive.
  2 ☐ She listened to all the examiner's points.
  3 ☐ She didn't manage to find a solution.
  4 ☐ She only considered Paul's career.
  5 ☐ She didn't ask any questions.
  6 ☐ She seemed genuinely interested in the problem.
  7 ☐ She has been to Australia.
  8 ☐ She knows Paul and Laura.

c Now in pairs do the same interactive task again, but try and ask different questions and find another solution.

11a Read the following prompts and in pairs identify:

  1 who the prompt is talking about – the examiner, a relative or a friend;
  2 where the problem/difficulty lies;
  3 the first question you might ask;
  4 how you might resolve the situation.

> **A** The other day I told a friend what I thought of her. Now I'm beginning to regret it.

> **B** My friend has just bought a beautiful, but very expensive dress. Now she's wondering if she really needs it.

> **C** I really wish I had taken a gap year before I went to university. I think I would have enjoyed it more as a result.

b Now role-play the prompts. One of you is the examiner and the other is the candidate.

Trinity TAKE AWAY

Examiner: What do you think **should be done** to encourage young people to start designing?
Candidate: They **could** hold competitions or give people the opportunity to display their designs in an exhibition.

1 Match the words (A-J) to the correct meanings (1-10).

A arson

B inmate

C cybercrime

D profile

E blog

F potential

G innovative

H outrageous

I impracticable

J starchitect

1 ☐ diary written online
2 ☐ capable of developing
3 ☐ an internationally acclaimed architect
4 ☐ not feasible
5 ☐ information about someone on a social networking site
6 ☐ expressing new ideas
7 ☐ person in prison
8 ☐ setting fire to a building
9 ☐ illegal activities on the Internet
10 ☐ shocking

2 Complete the following sentences using the correct form of the verb in brackets.

1 Yesterday Bernard Madoff .... after committing the biggest scam in history. (prosecute)

2 If she .... not .... her bank details on line, she .... a victim of identity theft. (give, be)

3 Armani .... a fashion designer if he hadn't been interested in clothes. (become)

4 More protection should .... to Internet users. (give)

5 Tougher laws should .... to stop cyber fraud. (introduce)

6 That must .... the bride. She's wearing a beautiful white dress. (be)

7 If I .... a laptop, I would work on the train to work. (have)

8 He .... Japanese, but he .... not .... it. (understand, speak)

3 Read the following comments and think of other ways of expressing the same idea.

0 It would be great to have a touch screen phone. Perhaps I'll get a Moon 8500.
   If I get a touch screen phone, I'll probably buy a Moon 8500

1 It might be a good idea to learn Spanish. Then I could work in South America.
   ....
   ....

2 I should apply for university. It would certainly open up more opportunities.
   ....
   ....

3 I'm in prison now as I was found guilty of identity fraud. How stupid I was!
   ....
   ....

4 Why don't they ban cars in city centres? It would certainly reduce pollution.
   ....
   ....

4 Which information refers to which part of the exam? Write T (Topic), I (Interactive), C (Conversation) or W (Whole Exam).

1 ☐ You need to take full responsibility for maintaining the interaction.

2 ☐ You should use functions and language of grade.

3 ☐ You should prepare for 6 subject areas.

4 ☐ You have to understand a prompt.

5 ☐ The examiner will ask you about 2 subject areas.

6 ☐ It isn't related to one of the subject areas for the conversation.

7 ☐ It's the first phase of the examination.

8 ☐ You should be interested in it.

9 ☐ You should prepare notes or a mind map.

10 ☐ It lasts 15 minutes.

5 Read the following interactive prompts and decide:

1 who the prompt is talking about – the examiner, a relative or a friend;

2 what decision was made;

3 the first question you might ask;

4 what the examiner might answer.

> **A** 'My best friend recently went on holiday with her family and really regretted it. It wasn't relaxing at all.'

> **B** 'When I was at school, I turned down the opportunity to study in the United States for a year. If I had gone, my life would be very different today.'

Exam tips

> Don't write out the topic in full. Don't memorise it.

> Make sure you prepare vocabulary and ideas for 6 subject areas for the Conversation phase.

> Listen carefully to the interactive prompt as it is important to understand every detail.

Units 1-3 Self-evaluation

Write Y (yes) or N (needs more practice) for each statement.

1 ☐ I can talk about technology.

2 ☐ I can talk about crime and punishment.

3 ☐ I can talk about design.

4 ☐ I can use grammar structures up to Trinity Grade 8.

5 ☐ I can use modal verbs with the passive.

6 ☐ I can use mixed conditionals.

Now you write 'can do' statements like the ones above for the interactive and communicative skills you have practised in Units 1-3.

REVIEW

Global
environmental issues

GRADE 9

Vocabulary

1a Look at the pictures and discuss these questions in pairs.

1 Which environmental problems do the pictures show?

2 How have these people's/animals' lives been affected by climate change?

3 How do you think they are feeling?

4 What would you do in these circumstances?

5 Who usually comes to the aid of people/ animals when these environmental issues occur?

b Have you seen circumstances like these in your country? In small groups talk about the climate change you have noticed in your own country and say if you think it has affected your daily life.

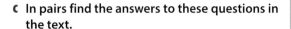

Reading

2a Look at the newspaper headlines below about climate change and discuss in pairs what they might mean.

> ### 40,000 BARRELS OF OIL A DAY GUSHING INTO GULF!

> ### WHERE HAVE ALL THE BEES GONE?

> ### CROP FAILURE SPELLS DISASTER

> ### SCIENTISTS REJECT GLOBAL COOLING

b Read the following text about climate change. In pairs decide which is the most appropriate headline from those above.

c In pairs find the answers to these questions in the text.

1 What effects do these polluting gases have on the planet?

2 Is it possible to remedy the situation quickly and why?

3 What is happening to the level of carbon dioxide in the atmosphere?

4 What kind of weather can we expect in the future?

d Now match a word (A-E) to its meaning (1-5).

A	greenhouse	**D**	drought
B	hurricane	**E**	heat wave
C	glacier		

1 ☐ period of unusually hot weather

2 ☐ mass of ice moving down a valley

3 ☐ very hot weather with insufficient water

4 ☐ glass building for growing plants

5 ☐ violent wind

Climate change or global warming is caused by increased levels of carbon dioxide and other polluting gases in the atmosphere. The gases trap heat by creating a blanket around the Earth, like the glass of a greenhouse. One of the main problems with the greenhouse gases is that once released they may stay in the atmosphere for up to 100 years. Therefore, even if we stopped emissions immediately, our weather would still be affected for some considerable time.

According to a recent report on climate change, concentrations of carbon dioxide in the atmosphere have been rising since the Industrial Revolution 250 years ago, and are currently at the highest level ever recorded. Scientists are particularly concerned that the rate of increase is beginning to accelerate. It is feared that as the planet gets warmer, the land and oceans will be less able to absorb the carbon dioxide. This will inevitably lead to a further temperature rise and more global warming.

In recent years, we have already witnessed the effects of this with rising sea levels, declining snow cover and retreating glaciers. More extreme weather is predicted with a greater risk of heat waves, drought, hurricanes and storms. These problems can only be tackled by reducing the amount of energy we use and investing in new environmentally-friendly technology. We should have done this a long time ago!

GRADE 9

Grammar focus

Should/might/could/must and the perfect infinitive

Look at this sentence from the article and answer the questions below.

We should have done this a long time ago.

1 Did we do anything about the situation?
2 Do we regret this now?

Should and the perfect infinitive is usually used to refer to something that was supposed to happen in the past but, in fact, didn't (often with the idea that it was the right thing to do).
We should have switched off the lights. We didn't need them.
I should have walked to work yesterday instead of driving.

Might and the perfect infinitive can be used when we are unsure about exactly what happened.
The factory looks empty. They might have closed it down because of the pollution.
There are very few flowers this summer. They might have died because of the hot weather.

Could and the perfect infinitive suggests a past opportunity or possibility that didn't materialise.
We could have stopped global warming many years ago, but nobody seemed to care.
They could have prevented the forest fire if it had been reported earlier.

Must and the perfect infinitive can be used when we are sure or can assume something has happened.
Where are all the birds? They must have died in the oil slick.
Many of the tropical rain forests have disappeared. They must have been chopped down.

3a **Complete each sentence with *should, might* or *could have*.**

0 Why did you drive so fast? You <u>should have</u> driven more slowly.

1 He is very seriously ill now. He .... gone to the doctor earlier.

2 I don't know why she didn't come. She .... stayed at home.

3 She .... worked in Los Angeles, but she wanted to stay in London.

4 John .... become a successful lawyer if he had continued his studies.

5 Why did you knock down that cyclist? You .... hurt her.

b **Now complete these sentences with *should/might/could/must* and the perfect infinitive.**

0 She didn't eat anything all day. She <u>should have eaten</u> something.

1 They didn't call the emergency services when the oil rig exploded. They ....

2 He was seriously injured. He ....

3 The environmental campaigner threw a stone at the policeman. He .... (not).

4 He resigned today so he ....

5 The sea isn't polluted at all now. It ....

c **Think of five examples about yourself and the environment.**

E.g. I could have used less water at home.

Listening

4a What do these words/phrases mean? Use a dictionary or ask your teacher.

> *carbon neutral   solar panels   wind turbine   triple glazing   compost   eco warrior   key worker   landfill*

b 🔊 Listen to Simon Grant, an engineer, talking about living in a carbon-neutral home. Answer the following questions.

1 Why did Simon want to live in a carbon-neutral home?
2 What is the house like in winter?
3 What does Simon have to do with his rubbish?
4 Are there any disadvantages?

c 🔊 Now listen again and decide if these statements are true (T), false (F) or don't know (DK).

1 ☐ He didn't care about environmental issues at all.
2 ☐ The rent is cheap.
3 ☐ The heating system is very effective.
4 ☐ The house is in the mountains.
5 ☐ Sorting out the rubbish takes some time.
6 ☐ The wind turbine is nice and quiet.

d Discuss in pairs if you would like to live in a carbon-neutral home.

Phonology

Intonation to convey attitude

🔊 Generally when we are enthusiastic and positive our voice goes high to show this.

A: I think my carbon-neutral home is great! ▲
B: It sounds amazing! ▲

When we are negative or unimpressed our voice goes down.
A: The oil spill in the Gulf of Mexico is terrible. ▼
B: Oh, it's absolutely awful. ▼

Sometimes the language is positive but the intonation is negative. This indicates you are being sarcastic or don't really like the information you have received.
A: The weather is going to be appalling this weekend. ▼
B: Wonderful! ▼

Good news = ▲ Bad news = ▼

5a 🔊 Listen to the following comments and mark either ▲ or ▼ according to whether the speaker's voice rises or falls.

1 Well done!
2 Terrible!
3 Excellent!
4 How terrible for you!
5 That sounds very interesting!
6 Great!

b Now in pairs practise the following with you voice going up or down as indicated.

1 Delicious! ▲
2 What an awful experience! ▼
3 Lovely weather! ▲
4 That's a terrible book! ▼
5 Sounds very boring! ▼
6 You lucky thing! ▲
7 Mmn ▲

Function focus
■ Evaluating past actions

6a Look at the mind map about things which have an impact on the environment and add more ideas.

b In pairs evaluate your past actions. Use the mind map to help you.

E.g. I always used to go to work by car.
I could have/should have used public transport.

I used to have a bath every night.
I must have wasted a lot of water.

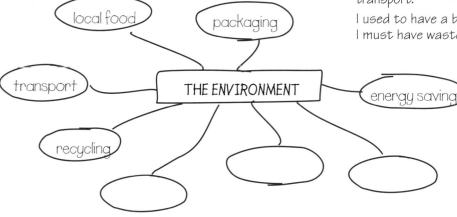

local food · packaging · transport · THE ENVIRONMENT · energy saving · recycling

exam EXPERT

Conversation phase
■ Responding to the Examiner

7 Complete the sentences (1-6) with an ending (A-F).

1 ☐ You need to prepare six subject areas
2 ☐ The examiner will ask you about
3 ☐ If you don't understand, don't worry,
4 ☐ If the examiner doesn't understand you,
5 ☐ If you need time to think,
6 ☐ Finally, don't forget to react

A try to give your views in a different way.
B ask the examiner to explain again.
C get used to using hesitation fillers.
D two of these subject areas.
E and respond appropriately.
F for the conversation phase.

8a 🔊 Listen to the recording and tick the phrases and expressions the candidate uses in the conversation with the examiner.

1   ....

  • Could you repeat that?
  • Sorry, I didn't quite catch that.
  • I didn't quite understand.
  • I'm not sure what you mean.
  • What exactly do you mean?

2   ....

  Time to think
  • Let me see.
  • Let me think about that.
  Uncertainty
  • I don't know about that.
  • I'm not sure really.
  Getting back to the subject
  • Anyway
  Filling the space
  • you know
  • sort of
  • well

3   ....

  • Really!
  • How interesting!
  • Absolutely!
  • How terrible!
  • I don't believe it!
  • I see.

b Now add one of the following titles to each group of words/phrases in a).

Hesitation fillers
Ways of coping with not understanding
Ways of reacting

c 🔊 Listen to the examiner and respond naturally to the prompts. Use the phrases above to help you.

Interactive phase

◼ Maintaining & developing the discourse

9a Complete the exam tips about the Interactive phase below with *Do* and *Don't*.

  1   .... let the examiner take control.

  2   .... listen carefully to what the examiner says.

  3   .... ask the examiner for more information.

  4   .... fire questions all the time!

  5   .... give a speech.

  6   .... use the functions of the grade.

b The conversation below is in the middle of an Interactive phase. Try and keep it going by responding appropriately.

Examiner: Actually, I'm terrified of flying.
Candidate: 1...
Examiner: I had a terrible experience once. I couldn't ever go on a plane again.
Candidate: 2...
Examiner: The plane had to make a crash landing.
Candidate: 3...
Examiner: Really! You feel the same?
Candidate: 4...
Examiner: That's quite a good idea. Wasn't the course frightening?
Candidate: 5...
Examiner: But what about all the environmental damage if I started flying on all my holidays?
Candidate: 6...

c Now in pairs use these prompts to develop a conversation.

  1   I've never been to Rome!

  2   My brother had a terrible experience!

  3   My teacher speaks 8 languages!

Trinity TAKE AWAY

Examiner: How **could you have been** more environmentally friendly when you were a child?
Candidate: Well, let me see... I **could have walked** to school instead of going in the car with my mum. I **must have contributed** lots of carbon dioxide to the atmosphere.

UNIT 5

Habits & obsessions

1 My husband is becoming totally obsessed with football. I have always known this and, in fact, our first date 10 years ago was going to watch Manchester United play Real Madrid.

Recently, however, I've become rather worried about him. He doesn't seem to want to do anything except watch football and now the World Cup is on, he barely speaks to me. He avidly reads all the football news in the papers every day and it has got to the point now when he really can't talk about anything else. I just wish he would realise there is more to life than football!

2 My daughter was really overweight from about the age of 10 and I know it was partly my fault for letting her eat more or less what she wanted. Anyway, it didn't seem to worry her until she was 16 and looking for an evening dress for the school leavers' ball. She couldn't find anything to fit her and decided to go on a diet. Within 2 months she had lost 5 kilos so we went out shopping together and found her a fabulous dress for the ball. She looked amazing and this boosted her confidence tremendously. I was a bit worried that she might continue with her diet and get too thin but we have had a chat about it and she has agreed just to eat healthily and only have the occasional cream cake or bar of chocolate.

3 I was recently appointed a director at our head office in New York. Of course I was highly delighted to get the job especially as I am still quite young, only 32, but it is proving to be more difficult than I had imagined. As a consequence, I am working really long hours, sometimes even sleeping in the office just to finish stuff off and even to demonstrate to my colleagues how committed I am. I work weekends, have absolutely no social life and am beginning to wonder whether it's all worth it. My friends say I'm a workaholic.

Reading

1a With a partner talk about your habits. How often you drink coffee, go shopping, eat chocolate, buy a lottery ticket and send texts? Are these obsessions?

b Read the letters (1-3) on the webpage and decide which are habits and which are obsessions. What's the difference?

c Read the following questions and in pairs express your opinions.

1 What are the three problems and which one is the most difficult to deal with?

2 What exactly is a workaholic? Can you think of other words ending in '-oholic'?

3 Why have people become so obsessed with dieting, exercise and physical appearance?

4 Is football just a game or is it more than that?

Singer Robbie Williams has been admitted to a US clinic for dependency on prescription drugs

Hey Big Spender

Katie Holmes, wife to Tom Cruise, spends $14 million in 6 months

'It's time to stub out my filthy smoking habit'

says England's goalkeeper David James

Vocabulary

2 Read the above headlines and discuss why celebrities – who apparently have everything in life – develop bad habits.

3a Make a list of your own habits and those of your friends and family.

b Look at your list and discuss in pairs which ones might develop into an obsession or even addiction. Is, for example, 'a chocaholic' just a fun term for someone who craves chocolate or something more serious?

Phonology

Stress in sentences

In English we tend to stress key words or the ones which are essential if you want to understand the meaning of the sentence. We don't usually stress pronouns (I/you/me), auxiliary and modal verbs (not main verbs), prepositions (at/on), conjunctions (and/but) or articles (a/the).

4 Read the following extract from the reading text and underline the words you think won't be stressed.

I was recently appointed a director at our head office in New York. Of course I was highly delighted to get the job especially as I am still quite young, only 32, but it is proving to be more difficult than I had imagined. As a consequence, I am working really long hours, sometimes even sleeping in the office just to finish stuff off and even to demonstrate to my colleagues how committed I am.

🔊 Now listen and see if you were right. Then practise reading the text with a partner.

GRADE 9

33

GRADE 9

Grammar focus

Wish, hope & if only

We use wish with the past simple, past perfect and would to express regret that things are not different and refer to situations that are unreal, unlikely or impossible.

Wish followed by the past simple is used to express a wish or regret about a situation in the present. Were is often used instead of was after I, he, she or it.
I wish I were thin.

Wish followed by *would* is used for a present or a future wish. It often expresses regret, dissatisfaction, impatience or irritation (you do not use this form to talk about yourself).
I just wish he would talk to me!

Wish followed by the past perfect is used for wishes or regrets about the past.
I wish I had never accepted the job.

If only can be used with the same tenses, but has a more emphatic meaning.
If only I had more will power!

Hope is used for wishes that seem possible in the future. Hope can be followed by the infinitive or a 'that' clause with the present or future.
I hope to go to university next year.
I just hope that she'll start a new life now.

5a Complete the following sentences with the correct form of the verb in brackets.

1 I love Venice! I wish I .... there now. (*be*)

2 He wishes he .... not .... smoking when he was young. (*start*)

3 If only he .... me. I can't wait to hear from him. (*ring*)

4 My football team are playing really badly. I just wish they .... (*improve*)

5 It was such a terrible party. I wish I .... at home. (*stay*)

6 You're so annoying. I wish you .... away. (*go*)

7 They hope .... to California next year. (*move*)

8 It was such an awful car accident. He wishes he .... not .... so fast. (*drive*)

9 I am rather overweight. I wish I .... thinner. (*be*)

10 You are a workaholic! I hope you .... a holiday soon. (*take*)

b Now make a new sentence for each situation, starting with 'I wish...', 'I hope...' or 'If only...'

1 I shouldn't have taken that job.
....

2 I simply can't remember his address.
....

3 I really would like him to get to work on time.
....

4 Why did I do something so stupid?
....

5 The weather in England is so awful!
....

Function focus

Expressing regrets, wishes and hopes

Sometimes we regret things that have happened in the past, we are not happy with our present situation or we would like to make changes in the future.
We may say:
If only I could win the lottery!
I should have gone to university.

I wish I lived in Shanghai.

I hope I'll get a better job next year.

6a Match the correct wish or regret (1-8) to the situation (A-H).

1. ☐ If only he would tell her.
2. ☐ I wish he had stayed.
3. ☐ I hope to move to Madrid.
4. ☐ I wish I hadn't shouted at him.
5. ☐ I should have worked harder.
6. ☐ I hope the doctor will come soon.
7. ☐ I wish I spoke more languages.
8. ☐ I wish I had travelled more.

A I have never been anywhere.
B The baby's got a very high temperature.
C I hardly did any work at university.
D I only speak English.
E She doesn't know he's married.
F I just lost my temper.
G I love Spain.
H He left so early.

b Look at the comments below and rephrase what the people are saying using the correct form of *wish*, *if only*, *hope* or *should*.

> 1 I hope my boss gets the sack!

> 2 I would love to fall in love and get married.

> 3 I often dream of travelling round South America.

> 4 What I did was absolutely stupid.

c Now in pairs think of two examples of the following:

1. your regrets about the past;
2. situations in the present you would like to change;
3. what you would like your friends and family to do in the future.

d Student A: turn to page 93 and read out the sentences. Student B: listen and answer.

Listening

7a In pairs think about your daily routine and habits, compare them and note down any differences. Then discuss how daily habits are affected by climate, job or studies and where you live.

b 🔊 Listen to this British family talking about their daily life. Who are the three people talking? What is their main problem?

c 🔊 Listen again. Make notes about the daily life of Jo, Mark and Eva. What might or must they be doing at these times?

0 It's 4.30 a.m.   *Jo must already be up.*

1 It's 8 a.m.   **4** It's 12.30 a.m.

2 It's 9 a.m.   **5** It's 5 p.m.

3 It's 11 a.m.

d In groups decide:

1 who you think has the easiest life and why;

2 how you think the children feel about their way of life;

3 how it differs from the way you were brought up as a child.

exam EXPERT

Interactive phase

◼ Using functions of the grade

8 Decide if the statements about the Interactive phase are true (T) or false (F).

1 ☐ The student talks until he can't think of anything else to say.

2 ☐ The student and examiner take turns in speaking.

3 ☐ You mustn't comment or ask the examiner questions.

4 ☐ You must tell the truth.

5 ☐ If the candidate doesn't keep the interaction going the phase will end.

9a Read the prompts (1-5) and discuss in pairs which functions (A-E) you might use in the subsequent Interactive phase.

A expressing regrets

B evaluating past actions

C hypothesising

D expressing wishes and hopes

E evaluating options

1 There was a fantastic job in the paper last week. I should have applied!

2 I can't decide where to go on holiday this year. I'd really like to try something completely different.

3 A very strange present was left on our doorstep last week. We really have no idea who it is from.

4 Sometimes I look back and wonder how my life could have been different.

5 One of the teachers at my school had a great influence on my decisions in life.

6 A friend of mine disappeared last year, but recently I received an email from her.

b Now try and think of a comment or question you could make for each prompt in a) using the function.

E.g. There was a fantastic job in the paper last week. I wish I'd applied for it.

Why do you wish you had applied for it?

Topic phase

■ Anticipating examiner questions

> Remember your topic should develop into a natural discussion, so you must try and think about the questions the examiner might ask you.

10a Look at the following examples of candidate and examiner exchange.

Candidate: There are many differences in attitude between people who live in the north and south of my country.
Examiner: That's interesting. Could you tell me a little more about these differences?
Candidate: Karate is an ancient form of martial arts which involves kata and kumite.
Examiner: Oh, I'm not sure what that means...

Now match the candidates' comments (1-5) to an appropriate examiner response (A-E).

1 ☐ Renaissance art was largely financed by the church or rulers of the day.

2 ☐ I think the words in Eminem's songs express his frustration.

3 ☐ I wish I could work in another country.

4 ☐ Mass immigration around the world could have both positive and negative consequences.

5 ☐ In my view, the scout movement plays an important role in young people's development.

A I see, so what exactly does he say?

B So where would you like to work?

C It sounds really important in your life. So how has it influenced you as you've been growing up?

D Why do you think they were interested in supporting these artists?

E So what do you think the positive consequences might be?

b Look at the following examples and try and predict the examiner's questions.

1 In my band we tend to play ska music.
   Examiner: ....?

2 My city has been badly affected by pollution.
   E: ....?

3 Many changes have taken place in society since my grandmother was young.
   E: ....?

4 If I were prime minister, I would certainly make some changes in my country.
   E: ....?

5 In my view, Italian food is the best in the world.
   E: ....?

c Now in pairs practise the topic you prepared in Unit 3. This time interrupt your partner by asking as many questions as possible.

Candidate: I **wish I lived** in a hot country.
Examiner: Really! How do you think your life would be different?

UNIT 6

Dreams & nightmares

Reading

1a With a partner talk about whether you ever have any dreams or nightmares. How often do you have them and what are they about?

b Now work in pairs. Student A reads A part of text and Student B reads B part. Close your book and explain briefly to your partner what you have learnt from the article. Is there any information which you find surprising?

Do we all dream?

Dreams are vivid episodes that occur in the mind while we sleep. Many people claim that they never dream but studies have shown that we all experience brain activity during sleep. You may of course not actually remember dreaming but this is not the same as not dreaming at all. Most people spend about two hours a night dreaming and this is usually in the final stage of the sleep cycle known as REM sleep. This stands for Rapid Eye Movement because in this stage of sleep your eyes move rapidly backwards and forwards under your eyelids.

It is not unusual for an individual to have multiple dreams during the night but we often forget having any of them. This is sometimes attributed to antibiotics, high stress levels or alcohol consumption or even too much or too little sleep. Many of us find it easy to recall a nightmare but forget having an enjoyable dream. This is because nightmares are often frightening and wake you up abruptly as a consequence. Furthermore, they usually take place in the early hours of the morning, shortly before you wake up, so you are more likely to remember them.

Why do we have dreams?

Experts disagree about the reasons for dreaming but it is commonly believed that dreams give us an opportunity to deal with issues unresolved during our daily lives. Dreams provide a safe outlet for expressing feelings and emotions which have been repressed. Many common dreams involve running away from danger, which may be a way of responding to threatening situations.

It is also thought that dreams are a biological necessity of sleep as it has been found that people who are woken up before they can dream are more stressed and irritable.

Dreaming a lot about the same person may simply indicate that someone is important in your life, but it may also reflect difficulties in that relationship that you refuse to accept.

Recurring dreams are a clear sign that something is not right and often reflect anxieties which need to be dealt with.

c Read the text again and in pairs answer the following questions.

1 What exactly are dreams?
2 What do we know from studies?
3 What exactly is REM?
4 Why do we often forget our dreams?
5 Why is it easier to remember nightmares?
6 How do dreams help us with our daily lives?
7 What happens if you don't have the opportunity to dream?
8 Is dreaming a lot about the same person a negative or positive sign?

Listening

2a 🔊 Look at the pictures. Have you ever dreamed about these things? Listen to Charlotte talking about her dream. What does she say about pictures A-C?

A

B

C

b 🔊 Listen again and answer these questions.

1 How does the weather contribute to her feelings both at home and in her dream?
2 Contrast her life at home with that on holiday.
3 Why is her lunch pink and cream?
4 How do you think she felt when she woke up?

Vocabulary

3a 🔊 Listen again and pick out 5 words which express something positive beginning with the following letters.

1 lux.................................
2 ele.................................
3 per.................................
4 won.................................
5 par.................................

b Now use the words from a) to complete the following sentences.

1 She looked so .... in a little black dress and neat string of pearls.
2 .... in a hot soapy bath is one of the great pleasures in life!
3 We stayed at the 7 star hotel in Dubai which can only be described as ....
4 Dinner was just .... It tasted delicious and the presentation was superb.
5 Wow! Your new boyfriend is really ....!

c Can you remember a pleasant dream you have had? Tell your partner about it using at least 5 positive adjectives.

GRADE 9

Grammar focus

Verbs followed by gerund and/or infinitive

Many verbs or expressions are followed by the gerund (verb + -ing) or infinitive (verb + to + infinitive) and some may be followed by both.
Look at the following sentences from the reading text.

You may of course not actually **remember dreaming**. (gerund after *remember*)

Many of us **forget having** an enjoyable dream but can remember nightmares. (gerund after *forget*)

But it may also reflect difficulties in the relationship that you **refuse to accept**. (infinitive after *refuse*)

4a Put the following verbs into the table.

> enjoy can't stand deny don't mind refuse
> avoid persuade consider suggest decide
> agree offer can't help

followed by gerund

followed by infinitive

b Complete the sentences using the correct form of the verbs above. There may be more than one appropriate answer.

1 I .... thinking about my nightmares.
2 She .... to tell her boyfriend about her amazing dream.
3 I .... eating junk food!
4 My friend .... going out for dinner.
5 John .... to apply for university.
6 In her dream Charlotte .... to marry Adonis.
7 The youth .... stealing the money.
8 I .... to go with her to the hospital.

5a Some verbs can be followed by either the gerund or the infinitive. What is the difference in meaning between the underlined parts in each pair?

1 **A** I <u>remember posting</u> the letter.
   B I <u>remembered to post</u> the letter.
2 **A** I was doing my homework, but I <u>stopped to watch</u> the football.
   B I <u>stopped watching</u> the football when the score was 5-0.

Don't forget that a verb after a preposition takes the gerund.
E.g.   I'm interested in learning English.

b Now complete the following sentences with the correct form of the verb in brackets.

1 I remember .... a nightmare about snakes. (have)
2 I'll never forget .... Angelina Jolie in a dream. (meet)
3 Try .... more exercise as an experiment. (take)
4 He stopped .... at us. (shout)
5 Don't forget .... me an email. (send)
6 Remember .... your passport with you. (take)

Function focus

Paraphrasing

During your interview you may need to paraphrase, that is to explain something again in another way to give greater clarity.

Read the passage below.
*In my dream I thought I was on a Caribbean island with the water lapping around my feet and the warmth of the sun sending me to sleep, but, in fact, I was startled to discover I **wasn't in the Caribbean** at all. Well, where was I? Somewhere in the north west of Scotland, a deserted island with sheep grazing and **a cold bracing wind**. How did I get it so wrong?*

The examiner might say:
How did you make a mistake like that?

You may respond by paraphrasing:
*The fact is that I **would have liked to have been on a Caribbean island**, but I was sitting on a **freezing beach** in Scotland, just dreaming.*

6a Now look at the examples on the right and write down how you might paraphrase each in one sentence.

b Now read through the sentences below, each of which represents a paraphrased version of a story. Then in pairs take turns to retell the story as you think it might have been originally.

1. The wedding went very well, apart from a few minor disasters in the morning.

2. Teachers in the UK have been subjected to so many changes in the educational system in recent years that they would really like a period of stability.

3. It is often claimed that domestic pets such as cats and dogs can be a great comfort, especially for the old and lonely.

1. The accident happened at about 8.30. Or was it 9? Anyway, I was having breakfast, reading the paper and so – oh, and then my son came down and he wanted a cup of coffee. Suddenly there was the most almighty crash, so I rushed outside to discover two cars in my garden. A woman was screaming and a man seemed to be trapped in the back of one of the cars.

2. A young child can acquire language in a variety of different ways. Naturally, the home environment is very important and the extent to which interaction takes place within the family. However, the extended family, friends, teachers, books and even television all have an important role to play.

3. The economy in Zanzibar is still largely dominated by agriculture and the fishing industry. In 1999, the economy showed great improvement and this was largely attributed to the increased production of cloves and clove products, which have sustained a good price on external markets.

Phonology

■ Intonation of question tags

Question tags are a useful way of involving the listener in what you are saying.
They are generally used:
A to give opinions or make comments;
B to check information.

When you are checking information, your voice goes up at the end because there is uncertainty. When you are giving opinions and making comments, you generally assume the listener agrees with you, and your voice falls at the end.

7a 🔊 **Listen and decide whether the statements are made for reason A or B above.**

1 It's a lovely day today, isn't it?
2 That film was terrible, wasn't it?
3 You've been to Paris, haven't you?
4 The train leaves in 10 minutes, doesn't it?
5 Cricket's terribly boring, isn't it?

🔊 **Now listen again and repeat.**

b 🔊 **Now listen to the candidate in the interview. Is her intonation falling or rising? Write F or R after each sentence.**

1 You come from England, don't you?
2 I think the family is very important, don't you?
3 I can look at my notes, can't I?
4 Obama is still the US president, isn't he?
5 Technology has changed our lives dramatically, hasn't it?

🔊 **Listen again and repeat.**

exam EXPERT

Topic phase

■ Engaging the examiner in the topic

The topic phase is not a monologue: you need to interact with the examiner.
If you have chosen a topic you are really interested in, then the examiner will respond to your enthusiasm. Your intonation is important.

8a Add question tags to the following statements.

1 People are becoming too obsessed with designer goods.
2 Twenty-five years ago, women used to stay at home and look after the family.
3 Global warming could soon become a very serious problem.
4 In the future, marriage will become less important.
5 Ballet is very physically demanding.

b Now write 3 question tags you could use for the topic you prepared in Unit 3. You should also try and ask the examiner questions.

9a Write some questions you could ask the examiner about the topics below. One question for each topic has been done for you.

1 **Football violence**
   Do you have this problem in your country?
   ....

2 **Junk food**
   Can you understand why junk food is so popular especially with young people?
   ....

3 **Size 0 models**
   Do you agree that we are all too concerned with our appearance?
   ....

4 **Lifelong learning**
   Do you think you are never too old to learn?
   ....

b Now write 3 questions you could ask the examiner about your topic.

Interactive phase

Exam practice

10a Read the following interactive task, underline key words and make sure you understand the situation.

> There is so much rubbish on television these days. There seem to be more and more reality TV shows like Big Brother. I wish they would show more interesting programmes.

Now note down the functional language you might need to use.

b Work in pairs. Student A is the examiner and Student B is the candidate. Student A: read out the following introduction to the phase and then the prompt in a).

For the next part, I'll tell you something. Then, you have to ask me questions to find out more information. You need to keep the conversation going. After about 4 minutes, I'll end the conversation. Are you ready?

Student B: start the interaction.

DON'T FORGET!

The candidate takes control. Both the candidate and the examiner make contributions – but the candidate's turns are longer. The phase lasts up to 4 minutes – it may finish earlier if the interaction is not maintained.

11 🔊 Listen to an example of the Interactive phase with the same prompt and discuss the questions below.

   1 Do the candidate and the examiner share the same views?

   2 Does the candidate win over the examiner?

   3 What points did you discuss in your discussion that weren't mentioned in the listening?

12a Now in groups of three do the prompt below.

> This Saturday I've been invited to two different weddings. I wish I could go to both but that would be difficult. I really don't know what to do as I don't want to offend anyone.

Student A is the examiner.

Student B is the candidate.

Student C takes notes on the interaction and make suggestions on possible improvements.

b Now practise the interactive tasks in pairs.

Student A: go to page 93.

Student B: go to page 94.

 **Trinity TAKE AWAY**

Candidate: I can't stand waking up when I'm having a really good dream in the morning, can you?
Examiner: Oh, I totally agree. But I remember feeling very relieved when I woke up from a nightmare!

REVIEW

1 Match the first half of each sentence (1-10) to the correct ending (A-J).

1 ☐ I remember
2 ☐ I failed all my exams so now I wish
3 ☐ He should have
4 ☐ He always avoided
5 ☐ They could
6 ☐ I wish I
7 ☐ They offered
8 ☐ He was advised
9 ☐ She's good at
10 ☐ I don't mind

A speaking foreign languages.
B arrived earlier.
C to see the doctor.
D lived in New York.
E eating junk food.
F I had worked harder.
G being on my own.
H to help the old man.
I seeing him last weekend.
J have been killed.

2 Complete the sentences with the words in the box.

> greenhouse workaholic confidence issues
> hurricane anxieties obsessed drought
> neutral luxuriating

1 .... gases may stay in the atmosphere for up to 100 years.
2 .... in Africa can lead to starvation.
3 Many people who are environmentally aware want to make their homes carbon ....
4 The .... swept through the Caribbean destroying towns and villages.
5 My husband works such long hours I'm beginning to think he's a ....
6 Many film stars are .... with their appearance.
7 Losing weight can boost your ....
8 Dreams give us the opportunity to deal with unresolved ....
9 Recurring dreams often reflect ....
10 .... in the sun's heat and radiance, I gazed up at the indigo sky.

3 Match the functions (A-G) to the sentences (1-7).

A Expressing abstract ideas
B Expressing regrets, wishes and hopes
C Evaluating past actions or course of events
D Expressing assumptions
E Hypothesising
F Evaluating options
G Paraphrasing

1 ☐ What I really meant to say was that the trip was a great experience.
2 ☐ It might be better to choose another course.
3 ☐ I wish I had accepted the job.
4 ☐ If cars were banned we might all get more exercise.
5 ☐ The exact nature of happiness is hard to define.
6 ☐ He could have helped his friend more when he was in trouble.
7 ☐ The birds must have died in the oil slick.

4 During the **Topic phase**, the examiner will ask you questions but it is very important that YOU ask the examiner questions too. Look at this list of student topics and decide what questions you could ask about them. Try and use Grade 9 functions and grammar.

0 Topic: My Ancestors
Do you wish you had researched your own family?

1 Topic: My favourite Film – *Twilight*

2 Topic: My Career as a Dancer

3 Topic: Friendship on the Internet

4 Topic: Sailing round the World

5 During the **Interactive phase** you must ask the examiner questions and make comments to find out more information.

0 Examiner: My two best friends have had a terrible argument.
You: *What was the argument about?*

1 I had a brilliant teacher at school.

2 I wish I lived in Australia.

3 The police went to the house next door last night.

4 My son has decided not to go to university.

6 In the Conversation phase the examiner will ask you questions about two Grade 9 subject areas. Think of a question you could ask the examiner about each subject.

0 Technology
Do you think computers should have been introduced into schools a long time ago?

1 Crime & punishment

2 Design

3 Global environmental issues

4 Habits & obsessions

5 Dreams & nightmares

Exam tip

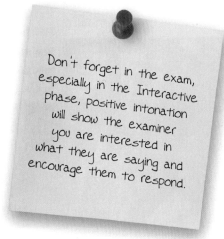

Don't forget in the exam, especially in the Interactive phase, positive intonation will show the examiner you are interested in what they are saying and encourage them to respond.

Units 4-6 Self-evaluation

Write Y (yes) or N (needs more practice) for each statement.

1 ☐ I can talk about global environmental issues.

2 ☐ I can talk about habits and obsessions.

3 ☐ I can talk about dreams and nightmares.

4 ☐ I can use modals with the perfect infinitive.

5 ☐ I can use *wish* and *hope*.

6 ☐ I can use gerunds and infinitives.

Now write 'can do' statements like the ones above for the interactive and communicative skills you have practised in Units 4-6.

REVIEW

Roles in the family (A)
Equal opportunities (B)

WHAT IS A TYPICAL UK FAMILY?

A

B

C

D

2	million lone-parent families
71%	headed by married couples
52%	own a pet
90%	of dads work and 68% of mums
79%	have a mortgage on their house

17	million families
1.8	average number of children per family
40%	of families have 2 cars
79%	have a mobile
65%	have a home computer

Vocabulary

■ Roles in the family

1 Look at the information above about a typical UK family in the early 21st century. Is there anything that surprises you? Discuss whether the UK picture reflects the situation in your own country and check on the Internet to find out.

2a Look at the pictures and talk about the family roles they represent. Who do you think has the most demanding role?

b Discuss what the following adjectives mean when used to describe families.

1 extended   3 traditional

2 nuclear   4 unconventional

c Compare the roles shown in the pictures with those in your family. Note down the differences and similarities and ask each other questions.

Student A: Does your own family bear any resemblance to any of the pictures?

Student B: Well, not really. Although we are a pretty conventional family, my mum and dad live together, my grandparents live a long way away in the south of the country.

d Discuss in groups to what extent roles in the family have changed in your lifetime. Do you think these changes have had a positive or negative effect? Give reasons.

Language focus

Idioms & expressions

Idioms are fixed expressions which can't be translated literally, so are sometimes rather difficult to understand. The context may help, however. In this example you may guess from the context that *under the weather* means *unwell*:

I'm feeling rather **under the weather** *today so I think I'll stay in bed.*

3a In pairs complete the gaps in the following expressions with one of the words in the box. Then discuss what they might mean.

> shoulder tears end swim blind
> chest head move talk mind

1 to be bored to ....
2 a .... to cry on
3 sink or ....
4 turn a .... eye to something
5 to my ....
6 small ....
7 get it off your ....
8 be at a loose ....
9 make a ....
10 laugh your .... off

b Now replace the phrase in bold with one of the expressions from a).

1 When my wife lost her job, I gave her **the support she needed when she was depressed**.

2 The lecture was absolutely awful. My friends and I just walked out because we were **really not interested at all**.

3 The comedian was brilliant. I **could not stop laughing**.

4 I think we have **to leave** now. It's getting late and the children have to go to bed.

5 It could go either way for her at university – **she might do well or just give it all up**.

6 My uncle behaved pretty badly at the party but I **pretended not to notice**.

Phonology

■ Using pauses and intonation to give clarity

In written English we use punctuation, which is expressed in spoken English with pauses and intonation. Pauses give us time to think and give the listener time to take in the information. Your voice will rise to introduce a new idea and fall to indicate the conclusion.

4a Listen to the news bulletin and mark the pauses (P), and rising (▲) and falling (▼) intonation.

'And now the news headlines.

Floods in Pakistan have left millions homeless and without running water. Charities are sending in emergency supplies as soon as weather conditions permit.

A man has been arrested in connection with a fire in Birmingham last night. He is thought to have been in the New Street area when the fire started.

And finally, the weather. Heavy rain will be moving in from the west.'

b Practise reading the headlines in pairs. Remember to use pauses and intonation.

Listening

■ Equal opportunities

5a 🔊 Listen to high-flying city graduate Sally Smith talking about her job in the city. How would you sum up Sally's experience working at the investment bank?

b 🔊 Listen again and answer the following questions.

1 Why did Sally take the job?

2 What do you think a 'golden hello' is?

3 What impressions did she get when she first started?

4 What effect did the working hours have on Sally?

5 How did her male colleagues behave towards her?

6 Do you think Sally made the right decision?

c 🔊 Now listen again and complete the sentences from the recording.

1 I had always been .... and, of course, getting a place at Oxford was ....

2 I was .... to be offered a job in the city ....

3 Well, you know, ... – sink or swim.

4 I knew I was good at my job, ..., if not better, but seemed ....

Now practise saying these sentences in pairs.

Reading

■ Equal opportunities

6a Simon, 39, has been in a wheelchair since he was 6. Before you read what Simon has to say, discuss the difficulties he might have experienced at the work place.

b Now read the text and discuss these questions.

1 What do the underlined parts of the text mean?

2 Which other groups of people may not experience equal opportunities? Why?

I have been in a wheel chair for most of my life and most of my experiences at work have been positive <u>although some companies have a long way to go</u>. My first employee <u>was very forward thinking for the time,</u> and made sure that all my needs were met and that I wasn't treated any differently from any other employee. My next job, however, was completely different. Nothing was set up conveniently for me and it was a constant challenge to get things changed. I also found I was excluded from certain meetings and <u>had decisions made over my head</u>. Eventually, I took them to an employment tribunal and won, <u>which was a huge boost to my confidence</u>.

Function focus

■ Developing an argument

7 In order to develop an argument you need to follow a process. Look at the list below (A-F) and number them (1-6) in the order you would do them.

A ☐ Talk it through with friends, family or teacher.

B ☐ Support your main points with concrete details or examples.

C ☐ Decide what your main arguments are going to be.

D ☐ Brainstorm every possible idea or argument.

E ☐ Select an idea to explore or defend.

F ☐ Come to a conclusion.

8 In the Conversation phase, the examiner might ask you about roles in the family. The examiner has selected the subject area/idea. He/she might say:

What do you think are the advantages and disadvantages of traditional family roles?

In pairs go through the process recommended above. Use a mind map to brainstorm. (*see also Unit 2 for mind maps*)

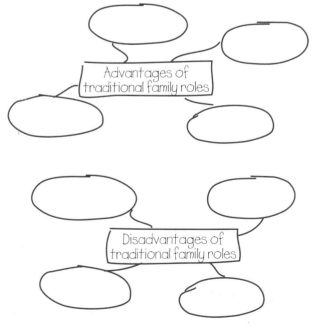

9a 🔊 26 Listen to what a candidate says in response to the question in exercise 8 and note down the two main advantages he mentions. (Remember, in the Conversation phase, you wouldn't take such a long turn as this. You have a natural conversation with the examiner.)

1 ....

2 ....

b Discuss in pairs any differences in the argument to your own. Then mention any criticisms of the candidate's arguments.

c 🔊 26 Listen again to the first and last parts of the listening and fill in the missing words. What is the important function of these missing words?

1 '......................, I think families organised in this way are much happier and more secure.'

2 '......................, I would like to say, that I grew up in a family like this and had a perfect childhood. ...., I would say a traditional family is definitely the best way to ensure happiness for your children.'

10 Now, on your own, work through the process above to answer the question.

Have equal opportunities been achieved in society today and in what areas have they still a long way to go?

When you have finished, practise developing your argument with a partner.

Conversation phase

■ Grade 10 subject areas

The Conversation phase involves a detailed discussion of two subject areas.
At Grade 10 the subject areas are provided in two different lists and are designed to take account of different levels of maturity. Your centre will decide which list is most appropriate. In Units 7-12 we will be looking at all these subjects. Don't forget your topic presentation cannot be taken from these lists.

List A (teenagers and less mature candidates)
Roles in the family
Communication
The school curriculum
Youth behaviour
Use of the Internet
Designer goods

List B (adults and more mature candidates)
International events
Equal opportunities
Social issues
The future of the planet
Scientific developments
Stress management

11a Now look at some of the subjects again. Write as many prompts as you can think of.

Roles in the family: *Grandparents*
Use of the Internet:
Equal opportunities:

b Now think of one question the examiner might ask you in the Conversation phase for each of your prompts.

Do you think grandparents should look after the children so that all mothers can go to work?

....
....
....
....
....

c Work in pairs practising your questions.

Listening phase

■ Introduction & exam practice

12a 27 🔊 Listen to a candidate talking about the Listening phase at Grade 10 and then decide whether the statements below are true (T) or false (F).

1 ☐ You will need to take notes.
2 ☐ There are two types of listening task.
3 ☐ There are two of Type 1 and two of Type 2.
4 ☐ The candidate may need to predict, deduce and infer.
5 ☐ Responses are very brief.
6 ☐ With Type 1 the candidate asks a question.
7 ☐ With Type 2 the candidate answers a question.
8 ☐ The examiner reads out the listening passage.

At the beginning of the Listening phase the examiner will say:
I'm going to read you three short passages and after I've finished each one, I would like you to either suggest a suitable ending or answer some questions. I'll then move on to the next passage.
Are you ready?

These two passages are incomplete. When I stop, I'd like you to tell me in just a few words how you think the passage finishes.

b In pairs read the following Type 1 tasks to each other. Talk about what has happened in the passage and what is likely to happen next. Decide what you are going to say to the examiner and then check the expected responses on page 93.

1 My best friend is a fantastic person and we get on incredibly well. We often meet up and discuss difficult issues in our lives or talk about our hopes and dreams for the future. To be honest, though, she has had a much more difficult life than me and has been rather bored at work. Imagine my delight when she called me the other day and said...

2 It had been the most terrible summer, rain every day, freezing cold and not even the shortest spell of sunshine. I was so depressed and spent every day browsing through holiday brochures and wondering where I could go and chill out on a sunny beach somewhere. Finally, I went to the travel agent and booked two weeks in Spain. What a relief! Then, to my irritation, as I drove to the airport...

The examiner then continues by saying:
After I've read the passage, I'll ask you about what you're heard.

c In pairs read the text to each other. Then discuss the answer to the question: consider the setting, the information about the people and what they were doing. Then check the answer on page 93.

It was an amazing weekend. The weather was great and I was with all my friends camping, cooking on an open fire and chatting into the early hours. The highlight of the event was seeing all my favourite bands play one after the other. It was absolutely brilliant and of course it was a perfect moment to see U2 in the flesh as it were!

Question: What was the event?

Examiner: What do you think are the advantages of traditional family roles?
Candidate: Well, I think families organised in this way provide a sense of security, but I would say that less conventional family groups can do this just as well.

UNIT 8

Use of the Internet (A)
Scientific developments (B)

A B C

D E F

Vocabulary

■ Use of the Internet

1a In pairs look at the pictures and discuss what the people might be using the Internet for.

b Look at the list of Internet functions below and tick (✓) which two are the most important and cross (✗) which two are least important for you. Then compare with a friend.

✓ 1 researching for school/university studies
  2 visiting chat rooms
  3 communicating by email (work/family/friends)
  4 shopping
✗ 5 finding websites that match interests and hobbies
  6 checking news/weather
  7 registering on social-networking website
✓ 8 booking flights/holidays
✗ 9 finding information on entertainment/ booking tickets
  10 listening to music

2 Match the words connected with computers and the Internet (A-J) to the meanings (1-10).

A click   F laptop
B trash   G bookmark
C surf   H attachment
D online   I contacts
E inbox   J search engine

1 ☐ be on the Internet
2 ☐ where unwanted emails are sent
3 ☐ a favourite website that you have saved
4 ☐ a file sent by email
5 ☐ move from website to website
6 ☐ a list of email addresses
7 ☐ where emails that you receive go
8 ☐ press a button on the mouse
9 ☐ a service that locates information
10 ☐ a portable computer

Listening

3a Discuss in pairs how you think older people might benefit from the Internet. Are there any older members of your family who have benefited from using the Internet?

b 🔊 Listen to Charles talking about the Internet. Try and guess how old he is. What factors helped you decide?

c 🔊 Listen again and answer the following questions.

1 What was Charles's initial reaction?
2 How did his friend Harry persuade him to change his mind?
3 How did he benefit from using email?
4 What information did he discover online?
5 What do you think a silver surfer is?

d Why do you think Irene decided to get the Internet installed? Discuss in pairs what difficulties you think older people might experience using the Internet.

e Before your next lesson use the Internet to research the most important scientific developments in the last 250 years. Your teacher will suggest some relevant websites.

Vocabulary

■ Scientific developments

4a Look at the pictures and discuss who you think these people are and what their contribution to science was.

b What do you think has been the most important scientific development in the last 250 years and why? Can you think of a prominent scientist in your own country?

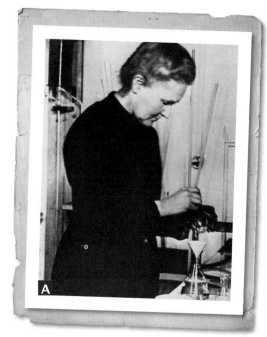

A

B

C

Reading

5a GM foods have been available since the 1990s. What does GM stand for? Are they available in your country?

b Read the text about genetically modified foods and underline 5 words that you would like to look up in your dictionary. After your first reading are you generally *for* or *against* GM foods?

c Read the text again and number the paragraphs in the correct order. What key words helped you decide?

d In pairs discuss the following questions.

1 What are the main arguments for GM food?

2 What are the main arguments against?

3 Discuss whether you have changed your views about GM food since reading the text in greater depth. What are your reasons?

WOULD YOU EAT THIS FOOD?

A ...... GM crops are produced by inserting genes from different plants or even animals to give it certain characteristics, such as resistance to pesticides. It is widely accepted in the US, but a controversial study suggesting GM potatoes might be toxic, provoked widespread opposition in Europe.

B ...... Opposition to GM crops rests largely on the premise that not enough is known about their long-term effects on the environment. It is feared that modified crops could become dangerous superweeds or accidentally breed with other plants which might genetically pollute the environment. What concerns people even more though, are the potential health risks. Firstly, interfering with genes in our food could produce dangerous toxins. Secondly, a potentially serious situation could develop if crops engineered to produce pharmaceutical drugs accidentally crossbreed with food varieties. There is, therefore, still uncertainty as to whether GM food is safe to eat and more research needs to be carried out to clarify this.

C ...... In conclusion, it is clear that despite doubts and serious fears about the long-term effects of GM foods, there are also benefits, especially in the Third World. There is, however, still an urgent need for more research and more concrete evidence to support the arguments, both for and against.

D ...... The issue of genetically modified (GM) food is highly controversial. It was supposed to be a new dawn for agriculture but, in fact, provoked a worldwide debate on the rights and wrongs of genetic engineering. If plants and vegetables could be tampered with, why not animals or even humans?

E ...... Despite these misgivings, there are keen supporters of GM foods, who argue that not only do they benefit the environment, but they can also prevent starvation in the Third World. There is less need for artificial chemicals and some varieties can thrive in very poor conditions helping poor farmers in these regions. Furthermore, some crops which have been vitamin or protein enhanced, can improve the health of the local people.

Language focus

Intensifiers

There are many ways of saying *very* and *really* but many of the alternatives only collocate with certain words and sound strange if used in other ways.

E.g. The issue of genetically modified food is **highly controversial**.

	Collates with
highly (often used with very positive words)	competitive, controversial, effective, likely, recommended, successful
absolutely, utterly (often used with very strong adjectives, when we can't use *very*)	brilliant, beautiful, convinced, devastated, furious, impossible, miserable, outrageous
deeply (often used with words expressing negative feelings)	concerned, hurt (feelings), shocked, sorry, unhappy
ridiculously (often suggesting something unacceptable or unbelievable)	big, early, easy, expensive, late, small
strongly (used with verbs to express opinions)	believe, endorse, object to, recommend, support
completely (used with some certain adjectives)	mad, different, stupid, ridiculous

6a Add these words to the most appropriate box in the table above.

appalled cheap profitable stupid pathetic to advise to oppose ashamed stunning amazing unusual upset

b Now complete the following sentences with an appropriate collocation from the table.

1   I do a lot of shopping at the market because it's ....
2   I was .... by the terrible things he said to me.
3   I .... GM food is dangerous.
4   Lucy had no problems passing the exam. She said it was ....
5   The government .... any move to ban smoking in public places.
6   We had a great holiday. It was ....
7   The young Oxford graduate became a .... city banker.
8   The bride looked .... at her wedding.

Phonology

■ Stress in longer words

At the advanced stage you will be using more complex vocabulary and it will certainly help you if you can use them confidently and without hesitation. A few general rules will help you although there are of course exceptions!

1 In words ending in *-ion, -ious, -ial*, the stress is on the syllable before.
E.g. contro'versial

2 Many words are stressed on the third to last syllable.
E.g. e'quality

3 The negative prefix of an adjective is not stressed.
E.g. un'certain

7a Can you think of one other example for each rule?

b 🔊 **Listen and write down the words you hear and mark the correct stress.**

School curriculum (A)
Stress management (B)

GRADE 10

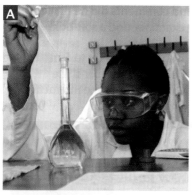

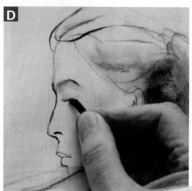

Vocabulary

■ School curriculum

1a There are 13 compulsory subjects for children aged 11 to 14 in England. Although academic subjects are still taught, there is a greater emphasis on learning practical and life skills than in some countries. Discuss in pairs what you these subjects are think they are and then check with your teacher. Use the pictures to help you. Then see page 94 to check if you were right.

b Now make a list of the school subjects in your country. Discuss whether there are currently any school subjects in your country which you think are irrelevant and any others which should be introduced.

Reading

2a In your opinion, does everyone speak English? What are the reasons for this? Skim the article and sum up the reasons why fewer UK students are learning foreign languages.

b Answer the following questions.

1 What could be the result of the decision to make foreign languages optional?

2 Why does the government feel it is better to concentrate on younger learners?

3 What does David White mean when he says 'it is about what we want a "rounded" person to be'?

4 How does the UK differ from most other European countries?

5 Does the writer agree with the UK policy?

c In pairs discuss these questions.

1 Do you think foreign languages should be compulsory from primary school?

2 Are languages likely to become more important in the future? Why?

3 What is the 'perfect' age to learn a language?

DOES EVERYONE REALLY SPEAK ENGLISH?

The perception that English is the most prevalent language in the world has meant that in the UK many young people fail to understand the need to learn a foreign language. Furthermore, the study of foreign languages in schools has been in sharp decline since the government made these subjects an optional part of the curriculum in secondary schools.

Many students have been overjoyed to have the opportunity to give up a subject they view as 'tedious'. However, it is feared that this could create a generation of monolingual teenagers unable to compete in an increasingly globalised market. The decision was made on the basis that it would be better to invest money in very young children with enthusiasm than force 15-year-olds to do something they are reluctant to do. Indeed, the government does intend to introduce language lessons into primary schools. Experiments have found that small children absorb language with amazing speed and enthusiasm, especially if the learning process is fun. Of course, this might be part of the problem. Secondary school language teaching may not be sufficiently stimulating to motivate the pupils and give them an understanding of the many opportunities a foreign language offers. There is, furthermore, the assumption that 'Everyone speaks English' so that it is perceived as a pointless exercise.

Many leading academics have expressed concern at the slump in the number of students studying languages at university. Professor David White, believes that learning a language is a 'core skill'.

'Compulsion may not generate hundreds of linguists but it is symbolic. It is about what we want a "rounded" person to be'. There is also concern that language learning is becoming increasingly the preserve of the middle classes because as state schools cut back, private schools are extending their provision by offering languages such as Chinese.

Without a doubt the UK is lagging behind other European countries in its approach in this field. It is estimated that 50% of young Europeans learn a foreign language from primary school and, with the exception of the UK, all students have to continue with a foreign language at least until the end of their compulsory education. In an enlarged and multilingual Europe this would seem to be a retrograde step which needs to be addressed as a matter of urgency.

GRADE 10

GRADE 10

Listening

■ Stress management

DON'T DO.

0800

262442

WE1465768

Language focus

■ Expressions used in conversation

4a Add the expressions to the table, to show their purpose in conversation.

> in fact   with regards to   as I was saying
> to tell you the truth   at any rate
> on the contrary   as a matter of fact
> you know   let me see

Returning to the main point anyway
Giving an opinion or expressing a feeling to be honest
For emphasis or contrast actually
Focusing on a particular point as for
Gaining time sort of

b Complete the following sentences with the most appropriate expressions from a). You may be able to use more than one.

1   .... to that financial report, could you give me some more relevant information?

2   ...., that is the end of the matter and I don't want you to refer to it again.

3   ...., I've thought about it quite carefully and I don't want to get involved in what I consider a rather risky venture.

4   You don't like Johnny Depp! Well, ..., I think he's absolutely fantastic!

5   .... before, youth crime is an important issue which needs to be addressed immediately.

c Use the expressions from a) to respond to these comments.

1 English is a difficult language, isn't it?

2 It's really not worth going to university.

3 In my view, learning a foreign language is a waste of time.

Function focus

■ Expressing beliefs

Many common verbs are used to express beliefs. In this context, they are usually used in the Present Simple.

5a In pairs look at the ways of expressing beliefs (1-8) and match them to as many of clauses A-H which are possible. Then compare your answers with the rest of the class.

D+F 1 I share your opinion ....

2 I'm absolutely convinced ....

3 I think ....

4 I firmly believe ....

5 I feel strongly ....

6 I'm a great believer in ....

7 I suspect ....

8 I've always maintained that ....

A equal opportunities are very important.

B on animal rights.

C that we should all try and save the planet.

D the man is innocent.

E he doesn't really love her.

F about the importance of the family.

G freedom of expression.

H teaching foreign languages at school.

b Put the expressions from a) in the appropriate column below.

very strong	I firmly believe
quite strong	
not very strong	

6a Look at the slogans at the bottom of the page and discuss what the people are protesting about.

0 testing cosmetics on animals

b Use the expressions in exercise 5 to imagine what the protestors might say to express their beliefs.

0 I feel strongly about animal rights...

c In pairs make up your own slogan and at least 3 sentences to express your beliefs.

0 STOP ANIMAL TESTING!

1 Make poverty history!

2 Clean up. Don't cover up!

3 JUSTICE FOR JUSTINE!

4 HOW MANY MORE ROADS!

5 PLANE CRAZY?

Topic phase

■ Preparing a formal p

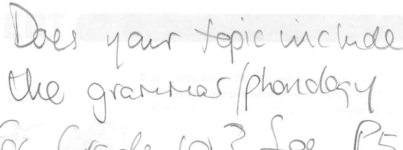

Does your topic include the grammar/phonology for Grade 10? See P5. Have you given examples?

7a 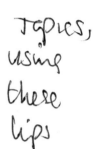 Listen to the beginning of two presentations and answer the following questions about each presentation.

1 Is the appropriate topic for Grade 10?

....

....

2 Is the appropriate language for Grade 10?

....

....

3 Is the presentation discursive?

....

....

4 Comment on the performance

....

....

b Discuss in pairs what is important when you make your presentation.

8a Make a list of 5 topic areas you feel might be appropriate for your presentation. Eliminate 3 by asking yourself the following questions.

1 Will I be able to speak for 5 minutes on this topic?

2 Will I be able to use the language of the grade?

3 Is the subject stimulating and likely to engage the examiner?

4 Will I be able to discuss this topic in the Discussion phase which follows?

5 Do I want to talk about this topic?

Giving an outline:
I will be examining...
I would like to concentr
I'd like to consider...
I'll explain how...

Topics, using these tips

Main content:
I'll start by...
I'll begin with...
Firstly...
Secondly...
My next point is...
Furthermore...

Conclusion:
Finally...
In conclusion...
To sum up...
I'd like to conclude by

9a Look again at the min prepared in exercise ε topics and make note four headings in the

b In pairs make up sentences using your and the signposting phrases.

Listening phase

■ Identifying context & participants

Type 2 listening requires the candidates to answer one question. This usually involves understanding the situation, place or people involved in the text.

10a In pairs read out the listening passage below and check the meaning of the words in bold. What place is being described?

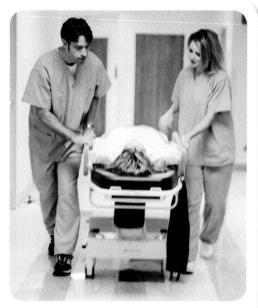

I had no idea if I was in the right place. There were a total of 15 floors and I had asked at reception which **ward** to go to but by now I had completely forgotten what they had said. There were so many people milling around, **visitors** mainly, although there might have been a few **patients** taking a walk. Of course, there were quite a lot of staff in **uniform** racing around and dealing with **emergencies**.

b Look at the following groups of words and identify the context.

1 website, chat, surfing, download, email

2 librarian, bookshelves, research, identity card, reference

3 waiting room, receptionist, stethoscope, magazines, examination

4 boots, referee, pitch, score, fans

5 documentary, presenter, weather forecast, reality programmes, soap opera

c Now do this activity with your class. The teacher will write a word on the board. One student sits so they cannot see the word. The rest of the class takes turns calling out a word associated with the one on the board and the student tries to guess what it is.

11a 35 🔊 **Listen to a student talking about exam stress. As you listen write down the key words that help you understand the situation.**

b Now predict what questions you think the examiner might ask you about this listening passage?

c 36 🔊 **Listen to these two listening tasks and answer the questions.**

What activity is the speaker describing?

Which words help you to understand the situation?

Candidate: My presentation today focuses on the problems of young people in my country. Here are some brief notes that I have prepared.
Examiner: Thank you.

1 Use the clues to complete the crossword.

Across

1 A subject which you have to study at school is ....

2 You feel .... when you haven't any friends to support you.

4 Most women expect equal .... at work.

7 You .... when you ride the waves or search the Internet.

8 When you do well, you have a sense of ....

9 Students need to do a lot of .... before exams.

Down

1 Many people don't agree about GM food. It is a .... issue.

3 You may send a document as an .... with your email.

5 If there is a drought, people may not have enough to eat and die of ....

6 A typical .... family has two children.

2 Complete the sentences with the words or phrases below.

> to be honest   ridiculously   anyway
> deeply   actually

1 The teacher is .... concerned about the student's progress.

2 That laptop is .... cheap.

3 .... I do like English food!

4 .... I'm absolutely hopeless at maths.

5 ...., let's get back to the important issue of the day.

3 Match the first part of the sentence (1-8) to the most appropriate second part (A-H).

1 ☐ The lecture was absolutely dreadful so

2 ☐ When my boyfriend and I split up I really needed

3 ☐ Mr Brown knew Simon was dishonest but he chose

4 ☐ Tony looked so funny dressed as a girl

5 ☐ It was impossible to have a meaningful conversation at the party so

6 ☐ Come on! We're going to miss the train if we don't

7 ☐ To be honest, now my exams are over,

8 ☐ Please can I talk to you because I really need to

A get something off my chest.

B I'm at a bit of a loose end.

C to turn a blind eye.

D that I just laughed my head off.

E we just made small talk.

F get a move on.

G a shoulder to cry on.

H we were bored to tears.

Type 1

4 In pairs practise reading the following listening prompts and discuss how you think each passage finishes.

1 We went out for the most amazing meal in a very stylish restaurant in town. We really splashed out as it was a special birthday. You can imagine how embarrassed we were when the bill arrived and we realised we'd forgotten to bring our...

2 I only just managed to get to the station on time. I rushed on to the platform, jumped on the train and grabbed a seat. I was so relieved to have made it. It was only when I started looking out of the window and saw unfamiliar places that I realised, to my horror, that I'd...

Type 2

5 In pairs read the following text to each other. Then discuss the answer to the question.

The shop offered me a free upgrade but I don't really want it. I think everyone's becoming far too obsessed with technology. Everywhere you go people are texting or you can hear ringtones. What's wrong with speaking to a person face-to-face?

Question: *What is the speaker talking about?*

6 Read the checklist about the topic presentation phase and decide whether the statements are true (T) or false (F).

1 ☐ You should prepare notes.

2 ☐ You don't give the notes to the examiner.

3 ☐ The examiner may take notes.

4 ☐ You mustn't choose a subject from the Conversation subject areas.

5 ☐ You can speak for up to 10 minutes.

6 ☐ The examiner will ask you questions during your presentation.

7 ☐ Written scripts are not allowed.

8 ☐ You should ask the examiner a question at the end of the presentation.

Exam tip

In the Listening phase make sure you listen carefully to the examiner so that you understand the situation or context and remember your answer may be only a few words.

Units 7-9 Self-evaluation

Write Y (yes) or N (needs more practice) for each statement.

1 ☐ I can talk about roles in the family and/or equal opportunities.

2 ☐ I can talk about the use of the Internet and/or scientific developments.

3 ☐ I can talk about the school curriculum and/or stress management.

4 ☐ I can use idioms and everyday expressions.

5 ☐ I can use intensifiers.

Now write 'can do' statements like the ones above for the interactive and communicative skills you have practised in Units 7-9.

Designer goods (A)
Future of the planet (B)

GRADE 10

Are designer goods a rip-off?

Trudging through the streets of any major city these days and you will see the familiar street vendors sorting out rows of identical handbags and trying to coax passers-by into making an impulse buy. All looks like complete tat of course. Who would want any of that stuff? Hang on though! Look at the designer brand names. That's pretty cheap. Just 10 euros. I could just be tempted.

So how could we possibly be duped into thinking a ten-euro bag from a street stall is anything like the real thing from a posh Milan store? Clearly, on closer inspection, anyone could see there is a difference. But does it matter? For just 10 euros, your friends might, just for a second, think you're stinking rich and have moved up a rung or two on the social ladder. And that's the key, isn't it? It's a rare moment when we too can join the world of celebrities, a kind of escapism if you like.

So if you actually had the cash, would it be worth investing in the odd designer number? Mmn, it would be a tricky decision – designer black dress or new car to get to work? Well, obviously the former would be better for the environment but is it a complete rip off? Well, if money was no object, why not? You're keeping a few highly profitable corporations in business and financing next season's catwalk creations.

And, of course, there really, really is a difference, isn't there? Those delicate fabrics, soft leathers and dresses to die for all represent the five-star luxury we crave.

On the other hand, isn't it all a bit obscene spending so much money on a fashion accessory? After all, there is still the most appalling poverty in some parts of the world, where the price of a designer handbag might well feed a family for a year or longer.

For goodness sake, have we no conscience at all?

Reading

■ Designer goods

1a In small groups find out if anyone has ever bought designer goods. If so, what did they buy and where from? Then decide if designer goods are really worth the money we pay for them. Why do people want to have designer goods?

b Read these comments made by two shoppers and decide if you agree with them or not.

'If the designer companies didn't charge so much, we wouldn't have to buy fakes.'

'Designer handbags or designer sunglasses are status symbols as long as no one knows they're fakes!'

c Skim through the text and decide what sort of publication this article might appear in. How would you describe the writer's style?

d Read the text again and complete the tables with the good and bad points mentioned.

FAKE DESIGNER GOODS	
good	**bad**

REAL DESIGNER GOODS	
good	**bad**

e Match the words and phrases (1-8) to the most appropriate meaning (A-H).

1	☐	tat	**A**	offensive
2	☐	coax	**B**	exploitation
3	☐	impulse	**C**	a narrow walkway
4	☐	trudging	**D**	rubbish
5	☐	rip off	**E**	persuade
6	☐	catwalk	**F**	without thinking
7	☐	obscene	**G**	walking heavily
8	☐	duped	**H**	deceived

Function focus

■ **Expressing opinions tentatively**

You may express opinions tentatively if:
1 you feel unsure about your opinions;
2 you need to be sensitive to other people's opinions;
3 you want to try and get other people's support.
We can say:

I may be wrong, but...   Don't you think...?
I suspect that...   I feel it could be...
It's possible...   I have my doubts, but...
I'm not totally
convinced, but I think...

2a In pairs change these strongly expressed opinions into tentative ones. The expressions may have to be adapted for the situation.

0 In my view, he's totally wrong!
I suspect he may be wrong

1 I'm convinced all politicians are corrupt.
....

2 I'm absolutely positive that the family is the foundation of society.
....

3 In my honest opinion, English food is terrible.
....

4 I do think community service is a better form of punishment than prison.
....

5 I really feel that young people today have a very easy life.
....

6 I've always maintained that compulsory education is a waste of time.
....

7 I really do think in special circumstances young people should be able to leave school before 18.
....

8 To my mind, she's made a big mistake.
....

b Now express your views tentatively about the following in pairs.

> *marriage vegetarianism religion military service diets designer clothes*

Reading

■ Future of the planet

3a Skim through the text and decide what sort of publication this article might appear in. How would you describe the writer's style? Do you think the style of this text or the one on page 66 would be most appropriate for your presentation?

b Read the text again and, in pairs, answer these questions.

1 What does the writer mean by 'consumerism and throwaway society'?

2 Why are people reluctant to change their lifestyle?

3 What kind of changes could they make?

4 What are the consequences of sending rubbish to a landfill site?

5 Why has the plastic bag come in for so much criticism?

6 Why do you think the Delhi project has been so successful?

c In groups 'dream up' your own idea for an environmentally-friendly business and report back to the rest of the class. Start off with a mind map.

MAKE MONEY AND SAVE THE PLANET!

In the current climate of consumerism and 'throwaway society', it is difficult to estimate how many of us consider the future of the planet in our daily lives. Global warming and the environment is thought to be a cause for concern, but very few people are prepared to drastically change their lifestyle for the sake of future generations. Recycling is an area to which most of us feel able to contribute. Organising our rubbish for recycling or taking bottles to the bottle bank is a task that can be fitted in around our daily routine. Despite fears that most of our rubbish will be transported across the world to a landfill site with few positive benefits for the environment, there is generally a greater awareness of the problem and acceptance of the need for action.

The plastic bag, so ubiquitous in modern-day society, has also become the subject of controversy. What was once considered so useful and so harmless, stuffed with books, shopping, rubbish or whatever, is now regarded with horror and disdain due to its lack of environmentally-friendly credentials. Supermarkets have been offering incentives to encourage the use of reusable or biodegradable bags and most plastic bags can now be recycled.

The most novel idea, however, has emerged perhaps from an unlikely source – India.

Plastic bags are collected from the Delhi slums by rag pickers who make their living scavenging through the rubbish. Then they take them home where they are moulded into sheets of plastic and stitched into attractively designed handbags which are then sent off to boutiques across the world. This project was the brainchild of an Indian couple Shalabh and Anita Ahuja who were amazed when the first few bags were snapped up. They seem to have discovered a winning formula that provides employment for local people, caters for designer tastes and more importantly shows respect for the future of the planet.

Grammar focus

The passive

The passive is often used to give a more formal, impersonal style to language.
It can therefore be used very effectively in your formal presentation. Look at this example from the second text.

'*...they are moulded into sheets of plastic and stitched into attractively designed handbags which are then sent off to boutiques around the world.*'

It is also used to give a generalised opinion.
'*Global warming is thought to be a cause for concern.*'

You can use a number of verbs in this way.
E.g. *expect, consider, believe, fear, suppose, say* and *allege.*

4a Rewrite the following sentences to give a generalised opinion.

0 Sea levels will definitely rise if we don't change our habits.

Sea levels *are expected to rise if we don't change our habits.* (*expect*)

1 In the newspapers it claims they got married last week.

They .... (*rumour*)

2 Many people think he is the greatest leader of all time.

He .... (*consider*)

3 They claim he stole all the money.

He .... (*allege*)

4 Apparently he had five wives that no one knew about!

He .... (*say*)

5 Everyone thinks he is very rich.

He .... (*believe*)

b Read the text below and fill in the gaps with an appropriate passive form. Use these verbs.

> set up   consider   expand   acclaim
> hand down   derive   establish

Valvona and Crolla, an Italian food store and wine merchant in Edinburgh, [1].................. by Benedetto Valvona from Cassino in the 1890s. It [2].................. originally .... to serve the tiny Italian immigrant community in the old town, but moved to its present site in 1934. It [3].................. now .... by many to be the best Italian food store in Britain. From its humble beginnings as a market stall, the business [4].................. in recent years by the younger members of the family and now boasts an Internet-shopping site as well as two restaurants which [5].................. widely .... by well-known foodies and restaurateurs. Many of the dishes [6].................. from recipes which [7].................. over the years by the family.

Phonology

■ Weak forms

Some words have a weak form /Ē/ and only have a strong form if they are at the beginning or end of a sentence or are being stressed for a particular reason. The following common words have a weak form:

a, an, and, are, at, can, am, for, had, have, has, of

6a 🔊 **Listen to the weak forms in these sentences. Then practise saying them.**

1 Come *and* meet him in my office.
2 They *are* not leaving until midday.
3 She's staying *at* home today.
4 They must *have* taken the train.
5 I *can* speak four languages.

b 🔊 **Now listen to the following sentences and fill in the gaps with the words you hear.**

1 I love fish .... chips.
2 Is this present .... me?
3 I would .... come if I .... known.
4 He's .... the cinema.
5 She .... speak six languages.

Listening

5a 🔊 **Listen to the news report and find out the reason for the protest at Heathrow airport.**

b 🔊 **Listen again. Are these statements true (T), false (F) or don't know (DK).**

1 ☐ The protestors want to stop the building of a new terminal.
2 ☐ People's houses will be destroyed if they build a new runway.
3 ☐ There are already four terminals.
4 ☐ The air aviation industry is 22% of the problem.
5 ☐ The demonstration will not be peaceful.
6 ☐ The airport is already under pressure.

exam EXPERT

Topic phase

■ Responding to the examiner

7a Read about the topic discussion phase and complete sentences 1-5 with A-E.

1 ☐ The discussion of the topic
2 ☐ The examiner only asks questions
3 ☐ The candidate should be pro-active
4 ☐ It is essential the candidate anticipates
5 ☐ The candidate should prepare

A possible answers.
B in the discussion.
C lasts 5 minutes.
D relating to the presentation.
E the examiner's questions.

b Read the extracts from topic presentations and, in pairs, prepare questions the examiner might ask.

0 Extract: Tourism on the south coast of Spain has developed in a different way to the rest of the country.

Possible examiner question: In what way is the development different?

1 As the number of old people increases, attitudes towards them have become more negative.

2 Communication through social-networking websites has a number of advantages.

3 In my view, worldwide rock concerts won't solve the problems of poverty in the Third World.

Listening phase

■ Anticipating what happens next

> **Type 1** Listening requires candidates to provide a suitable ending to two short texts they have heard. The responses will usually be only a few words, but the task will test high level listening skills such as predicting what will happen or deducing something.

8a In pairs look at the pictures on this page, and for each one discuss:

1 what is happening now;

2 what might have happened before;

3 what will happen next.

b In pairs read out the listening passage and discuss:

1 what the situation is;

2 what might have happened before;

3 what might happen after.

Well, we were determined, so we stayed there in the queue the entire night waiting for the ticket office to open. We just couldn't believe it. They are a brilliant team, of course, and have thousands of fans but this was ridiculous. The queue stretched for miles with everyone sporting team colours and chanting and singing. Then the ticket office opened and eventually we got to front of the queue, but to our horror we found...

c [🔊 40] **Listen to four incomplete passages. Suggest a possible ending for each.**

Trinity TAKE AWAY

Examiner: How do you feel about fake designer goods?
Candidate: I'm not totally convinced that they are a good thing because they encourage people to use clothes and accessories to show off, but generally I think they offer excellent value for the consumer.

GRADE 10

Communication (A)
Social issues (B)

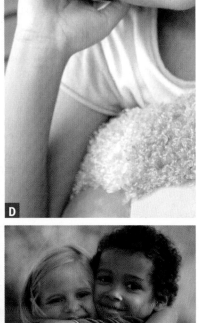

A   B   C   D   E   F   G

Vocabulary

■ Communication

1a Look at the pictures and discuss these questions in pairs.

1 How are these people communicating with each other?
2 What are the differences between face-to-face communication and communication via technology?
3 What is the role of body language in communicating?
4 In what way has communication changed over the years?
5 What are the qualities of a good communicator?

b Now think of two more questions to ask each other about communication.

H

Function focus

■ **Summarising arguments & ideas**

2  Listen to the extract from the conversation phase and summarise what the candidate says about how technology has changed the way we communicate.

....

....

....

3a Summarising skills can be useful in the different phases of the exam. Match a phase of the exam (A-E) to each sentence (1-5).

A Topic presentation

B Topic discussion

C Interactive phase

D Listening

E Conversation

Summarising skills are...

0 ☑ D useful in Type 2.

1 ☐ useful to summarise ideas and information.

2 ☐ useful when summing up ideas and opinions.

3 ☐ useful when reviewing ideas expressed in the presentation.

4 ☐ useful when researching.

5 ☐ useful to make notes to give to the examiner.

b Make brief notes about your life from when you were born until the present.

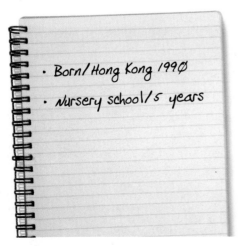

- Born / Hong Kong 1990
- Nursery school / 5 years

c In pairs recount your life story for 2 minutes only.

Reading

■ **Social issues**

4a Make a list of social issues affecting your country at the moment. Compare your list with your partner's and discuss the reason for them.

b Student A reads about Toby below and Student B about Camilla on page 74. Tell each other about the person you have just read about.

Toby is only 13 and has been caring for his mother for over 2 years. She had meningitis some years ago and now suffers severe memory loss and his father is disabled. They do have some help from social services, but as soon as Toby gets back from school his 'real' work day starts. He does the shopping, clears up, cooks the dinner and helps his parents get ready for bed. He rarely goes out to play with his friends and is struggling to cope with his responsibilities. Toby admits to often crying himself to sleep because he is so tired and exhausted. He is showing signs of depression.

GRADE 10

Camilla is a 25-year-old History graduate. She had always been a good student and had never doubted she would make a success of her life. However, when she started applying for jobs she started to realise how difficult it was. She was keen to develop a career in journalism or television, but there always seemed to be hundreds of applicants for every job. After three years of casual work in bars and restaurants trying to make ends meet, she was beginning to give up hope. Then one day she glanced at the local paper and saw a job advertised working for the local TV station. 'One last attempt!' she muttered. And to her delight she got the job.

c **Camilla has managed to resolve her problems but Toby still needs help. In pairs work out a plan for him with suggestions for dealing with his situation.**

Listening

5a **Look these words up in your dictionary or ask your teacher.**

> cosmopolitan   a float   eclectic
> leaking   kaleidoscope

b 🔊 **Listen to this report about how immigration has changed London. What impressions do you get of the city?**

c 🔊 **Listen again and complete the sentences.**

1   The reporter's family moved from .... to England in the '50s.

2   Soho is possibly the most .... area of London.

3   At Chinese New Year there are colourful .... and dragon and lion ....

4   The Notting Hill Carnival celebrates the .... and .... of the Caribbean.

5   Indians and Pakistanis moved to Southall because of its .... to Heathrow airport.

6   Chicken Tikka Massala is often .... the British national dish.

7   Eastern European immigrants fill the .... in the .... market.

8   They make a valuable .... to London's rich kaleidoscope.

d **In groups discuss these questions.**

1   What problems do you think immigrants have when they first arrive in a new country?

2   What can the local community do to help them?

Language focus

Intensifiers

In Unit 8 we looked at the most common intensifiers (*highly*, *absolutely* etc). Now we are going to look at intensifiers which tend to collocate with a particular adjective.

E.g. *Jenny got hopelessly lost in New York.*

6a Read the words below (1-6) and match each one to the most appropriate adjective (A-F).

1 ☐	seriously	**A**	beautiful
2 ☐	greatly	**B**	different
3 ☐	radically	**C**	impossible
4 ☐	virtually	**D**	injured
5 ☐	dimly	**E**	exaggerated
6 ☐	strikingly	**F**	lit

b Now use the collocations from a) to make sentences.

E.g. *The university library was **dimly lit**.*

Modifiers

Modifiers are different to intensifiers; they are used to make nouns and adverbs less intense in meaning. These are the most common modifiers.

fairly – weakest   *quite* – slightly stronger
rather and *pretty* – the strongest

Your intonation will indicate a great deal.
*He's **rather** nice* (said with great enthusiasm)
= you really like him.
*He's **rather** nice* (said in an indifferent way)
= you think he's alright.

Other common modifiers are *reasonably*, *mildly*, *moderately*, *basically* and *certainly*.

7 Disagree with what the speaker says by using a modifier and change the adjective.

0 **A** I think he's highly intelligent.
    B *Oh, I think he's rather stupid/unintelligent.*
    ....

00 **A** That woman is strikingly beautiful.
    B *Oh, I think she's pretty ugly.*
    ....

1 **A** The film was absolutely brilliant.
    B ....

2 **A** That joke was really funny.
    B ....

3 **A** The Indian restaurant in town is extremely expensive.
    B ....

4 **A** The building is radically different.
    B ....

Phonology

■ Intonation of intensifiers and modifiers

8a 🔊 **Listen to these people talking. What do you notice about the intonation of adjectives with modifiers and intensifiers?**

In general, when we use intensifiers our intonation goes up although if the subject matter is serious it may remain flat. When we use modifiers our voice usually remains flat. Sometimes, however, we can make modifiers more enthusiastic by using a higher tone.

E.g. 🔊 *I thought it was rather good.*
I thought it was quite good.

b 🔊 **Listen to the sentences and decide if the intonation is flat (F) or high (H).**

1 ☐ The crossword was virtually impossible to do.
2 ☐ The story was greatly exaggerated in the newspapers.
3 ☐ I thought that book was rather boring.
4 ☐ She was seriously injured in the car crash.
5 ☐ That dress is extremely expensive.
6 ☐ This exercise is fairly difficult.

Now in pairs practice saying the sentences with the appropriate intonation.

exam EXPERT

Conversation phase

■ Sharing responsibility

You need to be prepared to discuss any of the subject areas (from List A or B, but not both). However, the examiner will only ask about two of them. At Grade 10 you will need to be pro-active and share responsibility for the direction and flow, not simply answer the examiner's questions.

9 In pairs discuss the prompts below and use your own ideas to complete the table.

List A Subject Areas	Prompt	Examiner prompts/questions	Candidate response/question
Roles in the family	Working mothers	What difficulties might you experience as a working mother/parent?	I suppose it could be difficult at times to balance family life and work. Would you agree?
School curriculum	Changes to curriculum	If you were head teacher, what subjects would you introduce into your school?	Well, actually, I would bring in subjects that helped the kids with life skills. Life skills are often more difficult than academic subjects, aren't they?
Youth behaviour	Bad behaviour	1	Quite honestly, I think bad behaviour is often due to boredom.
Use of the Internet	Advantages	What do you think are the advantages of the Internet?	2
Communication	Communicating with body language	3	4
Designer goods	Exploitation of the consumer	5	6

10a Choose a subject area and in pairs practice the conversation phase using the prompts from the table to help you.

b Read through List B subject areas and think of a question you could ask the examiner about each of these subjects.

E.g. **International events**: *If you had the chance, what major international event would you like to attend?*

International events

Equal opportunities

Social issues

The future of the planet

Scientific developments

Stress management

Interactive phase
■ Using functions of the grade

11a Read the interactive prompts in the speech bubbles and decide which of the grade 10 functions (A-F) you are most likely to use for each one.

A Developing an argument

B Defending a point of view

C Expressing beliefs

D Expressing opinions tentatively

E Summarising information, ideas and arguments

F Deducing

b In pairs practise the prompts using the appropriate functions. Student A is the examiner, student B is the candidate.

c Now swap roles.

d In pairs write out a prompt of your own on a piece of paper. Exchange your prompt with the pair beside you. Discuss how easy/difficult you would find it as the candidate and what techniques you would use to keep the interaction going.

¹ I went to see a film the other day which had had rave reviews in the press. Actually, I don't know why because I thought it was pretty awful.

² My 18-year-old son is going travelling round the world for 6 months before he goes to university. We have had some quite serious arguments about the value of this trip and to be honest he has some valid reasons for doing it, but I am really quite worried about it all.

³ It is often thought that sport is a brilliant way of teaching children all sorts of different skills, but I must admit that I'm not totally convinced. It could end up with children feeling totally humiliated.

⁴ My best friend is getting married next month to someone years younger than her. I don't like him much and am rather suspicious of his motives, but I'm not sure if I should say anything.

Trinity TAKE AWAY

Examiner: I wasn't quite sure what you meant when you said people have lost the art of communication.

Candidate: Well, actually I meant that when we communicate by text or email, we don't express our ideas clearly enough.

Youth behaviour (A)
International events (B)

THE GAP YEAR EXPERIENCE

An increasing number of young people in the UK are opting for a gap year spent either travelling or working abroad before they go to university. It is often seen as an opportunity to see the world and have fun, but more recently young volunteers have decided to help communities worldwide by participating in local projects.

Vocabulary

■ Youth behaviour

1a **In pairs look at the photos above and answer the questions.**

1 What do you think volunteers do in these places?

2 Why do young people want to get involved in these projects?

3 Do you think the communities there really benefit?

4 In what way is volunteering in a community abroad different to travelling around the world?

b 🔊 **Listen to Lucy talking about her experiences in Rio and answer these questions.**

1 What kind of work was she doing?

2 What experiences did she have?

3 How did she feel about it all?

2 **In groups discuss how young people behave in your area and give examples of both the positive and negative effects they have on the community.**

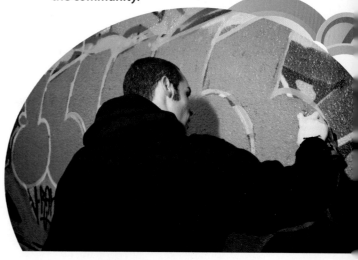

Reading

■ International events

3a Discuss in pairs what you think an international event is. Make a list of all international events you can think of and compare your list with another student. Find out if anyone has ever attended an international event.

b Discuss in groups how far you agree with Peter Gabriel's view on the power of music.

c In pairs answer these questions.

1 How would you describe the atmosphere at this event?

2 How do you know that the audience were enjoying the event?

3 If you had gone to the festival, what would you have enjoyed the most?

4 In what way was this 'a truly international event'?

WOMAD

❝ The festivals have allowed many different audiences to gain an insight into cultures other than their own through the enjoyment of music. Music is a universal language, it draws people together and proves, as well as anything, the stupidity of racism. ❞

Peter Gabriel, co-founder of WOMAD and rock singer

WOMAD stands for World of Music, Arts and Dance, a unique music festival that brings together artists from all around the world to celebrate a variety of musical styles and cultural identities. Since the first festival in the UK in 1982 WOMAD has held more than 160 festivals in 27 countries including Abu Dhabi, New Zealand, Estonia, Spain, Italy, Turkey and Japan. Over the years, thousands of artists must have performed to an audience of millions.

At the 2010 UK WOMAD festival 'the glorious sounds of Africa' reverberated around the beautiful setting of rural England on a summer's day. Malian Afro-pop star Salif Keita was headlining while the crowd welcomed the sensational rhythms of the Drummers of Burundi with a frenzy of cheering and clapping. A truly international event unfolded as 100 artists from far-flung continents captivated their enthusiastic audience and seemed to make the world a smaller place.

WOMAD is not only about the music, however, as the festival site itself boasts a huge array of stalls and cafes as well as entertainment for all the family. You can sit on the grass sampling the gastronomic delights of Thailand, India or Italy, buy yourself a Bob Marley T-shirt or try on hats and exotic jewellery from places you may never have even heard of. Children have the freedom to run around, jump on the trampoline or create magnificent plasticine models at one of the workshops. Meanwhile, back at the campsite, families chill out, loll on their sleeping bags or cook dinner over an open fire before being lured back to the distant drum beat. Here in a field in England you have the opportunity to experience an astonishing mix of tastes, sounds and cultures without even venturing near the airport!

GRADE 10

Function focus

■ Deducing & expressing assumptions

Sometimes we don't know the truth or actual facts about a situation but we can deduce or assume something from what we observe or even guess.

Example 1

When we listen to Lucy talking about her experiences in Brazil, we might say:
It **must have** been a challenge for her. (past assumption)
I **suppose** it was a challenge for her.

Example 2

We can also say about the audience at WOMAD:
They **must** love music.
I **assume** they love music.

Example 3

When we deduce that something is impossible we can say:
She **can't** have much money. She's unemployed.
He **can't have** gone far. He's left his car in the garage.

4 Complete the sentences to make deductions using a suitable verb.

0 She owns a car. She ..<u>must have</u>.. a driving licence.

1 Jo .... very disappointed when she failed the exam.

2 You .... lost the keys! They were on the table a few seconds ago.

3 This .... his house. It's far too big.

4 He has taken his passport. He .... the country.

5 Mum's not at the office, so she .... at home.

5a A robbery has taken place at a remote farmhouse where an elderly man, Bill Jones, lives. Detective Inspector James sends his team to the scene to gather as much information as possible for him. Detective Inspector James reads the notes and makes some assumptions.

> E.g. The intruder came by bicycle. He must live nearby. He can't be far away.

Now continue making as many sentences as you can using the notes in the policeman's notebook.

b You are at school/work now. In pairs imagine what your family and friends must be doing.

> E.g. My dad must be driving to work. My sister can't be at home.

Language focus

■ Signposting words

6a Signposting words are an important way of indicating to the examiner the direction and structure of your arguments. Look at the table on the right and add phrases to each function.

b Now check that you have included appropriate signposting phrases in the presentation you have prepared for the examination.

Function	Language
Introducing	Firstly To begin with 1......................
Moving on	Secondly Turning to 2......................
Adding	In addition Furthermore 3......................
Concluding	In conclusion To sum up 4......................

Topic phase

■ Presentation & discussion

7a 🔊 Listen to the first part of a candidate's presentation and then decide if the comments below are true (T) or false (F).

1. ☐ The candidate gave the examiner her notes.
2. ☐ She rushed the presentation.
3. ☐ She had clearly memorised the presentation.
4. ☐ There wasn't a clear structure.

exam EXPERT

b What was your overall impression of the candidate's performance?

8a You should have prepared your own presentation by now. Work in pairs.

Student A: give your presentation and then complete Score Card A to check on your performance. Give yourself one point for every sentence (1-5) with which you agree and deduct one point from every sentence (A-E) with which you agree. How many points did you get?

Student B: complete Score Card B (see page 94) and then compare notes with Student A to see if you agree.

Now make any necessary improvements. Then swap roles.

b Why do you think it is important to enjoy giving your presentation?

c Give your presentation again making sure you hand your partner your notes. Your partner makes notes too and then initiates the topic discussion phase.

Score card A

1. ☐ I enjoyed giving the presentation.
2. ☐ I spoke for five minutes.
3. ☐ I made eye contact with the examiner.
4. ☐ My presentation had a clear structure.
5. ☐ I gave the examiner my notes.

A. ☐ I memorised the presentation.
B. ☐ I had too much material.
C. ☐ I rushed the presentation and finished early.
D. ☐ I didn't enjoy giving the presentation.
E. ☐ I didn't bring any notes.

Interactive phase

■ Exam practice

Don't forget the candidate is responsible for developing the interaction. The examiner will conclude this phase early if that fails to happen.

9 Practise the following Interactive tasks. Your teacher or partner should read out the instructions below and then a prompt (1-5). Then you should develop the interaction by asking questions or making comments about the prompt.

Instructions:

*In this task, I'll start by telling you something. You'll have to ask me questions to find out more information. It's **your** responsibility to maintain the conversation. Are you ready?*

Prompts:

1 Recently I made a decision which I think might have been a big mistake. I lent a lot of money to a friend of mine.

2 My friend claims she has 215 friends on a social networking site but I'm not sure that this is real friendship.

3 My elderly uncle is rather old and forgetful now and I really don't know what we should do about the situation.

4 My friend's daughter has just returned from her gap year and has just told her parents she doesn't want to go to university anymore. They are furious but maybe she's right.

5 I used to think all these theories about the meaning of dreams were complete rubbish but having heard a friend's story, I'm not so sure.

Listening phase

■ Exam practice

10a **Practise the following listening texts. Your teacher or partner should read out the instructions then the passages. In pairs do the three below.**

I'm going to read you three short passages and after I've finished each one, I would like you to either suggest a suitable ending or answer some questions. I'll then move on to the next passage. Are you ready?

These two passages are incomplete. When I stop, I'd like you to tell me in just a few words how you think the passage finishes.

1 We had been so looking forward to our holiday. The hotel looked absolutely fantastic in the brochure, beautiful gardens, swimming pool and so on. You can imagine how disappointed we were when we arrived and were told...

2 There was a car accident outside our house the other day. I was watching from my living room window when it happened and an old lady was knocked down. She seemed alright, just a bit shocked, but I was stunned when the driver of the car just...

After I've read this passage, I'll ask you about such things as the context and people involved.

3 Everyone was in a hurry racing around in different directions. I looked up at the board and could see there was one in 20 minutes. That wasn't too bad. The platform wasn't up yet but it would probably say shortly. I decided to pop over to the kiosk for a cup of coffee.

Where is the speaker?

b **Listen to the two Type 1 tasks from another listening task and complete it in pairs.**

 Type 1, task 1

 Type 1, task 2

c Now listen and complete the Type 2 task.

Conversation phase

■ Exam practice

11 In pairs write down the subject areas for
List A or B on small pieces of paper and put
them in a hat or bag. Take turns in taking
out a piece of paper and start talking about
the subject area. Your partner should join in
at the earliest opportunity.

List A

Roles in the family
Communication
The school curriculum
Youth behaviour
Use of the Internet
Designer goods

List B

International events
Equal opportunities
Social issues
The future of the planet
Scientific developments
Stress management

Trinity TAKE AWAY

Examiner: I went to the WOMAD festival last weekend.
Candidate: Really! It **must have** been fantastic. I **suppose** you tried lots of delicious food
from different countries and I **bet** you met lots of interesting people too. Which was your
favourite band?

Review Units 10-12

1 Check you understand these words from units 10-12. Then write a sentence using each one.

Unit 10

0 fake I often buy fake designer handbags if I see one I really like

1 catwalk ....

2 appalling ....

X **3** ubiquitous ....

X **4** biodegradable ....

5 rip off ....

Unit 11

X **6** depression ....

X **7** exhausted ....

X **8** mutter ....

9 eclectic ....

10 cosmopolitan ....

Unit 12

11 volunteer ....

12 poverty ....

13 insight ....

14 reverberate ....

15 frenzy ....

2 Complete the sentences with a suitable verb and/or phrase. You may want to refer to the grammar and language focus sections in this book.

1 I wish you .... making so much noise.

2 It is .... that 200 people have died in the earthquake.

3 If I .... you were coming, I would have prepared dinner for everyone.

4 The man has .... to 10 years in prison.

5 Your exam results are disappointing. You really .... worked harder!

6 He is lucky to be alive. He .... killed.

7 My parents .... lived in this town since they were born.

8 I usually .... eating very fatty food.

9 He comes from St Petersburg so he .... be Russian.

10 If only I .... more money!

11 Her teacher .... her to go to university.

12 If I .... you, I would take a gap year.

13 Those designer clothes are .... expensive.

14 Well, ..., let's get back to the important issues.

15 The 2010 WOMAD festival was .... brilliant!

16 It was .... impossible to understand what he was saying.

17 The church .... by a famous architect in the early 19th century.

18 I don't know if Marie will survive in New York. She'll either .... or swim.

List B

5. What do you think are the most important causes of stress these days?

6. What do you consider to be the most pressing social problems in your country?

7. What measures should every individual take to help save the planet?

8. Which scientific development has been the most significant in the last 50 years?

Now in pairs ask each other these questions.

What do you need to do now?

1. Decide on your topic for your presentation.
2. Prepare a mind map and start researching your presentation.
3. Revise the functions and grammar for Grade 10.
4. Practice the Listening and Interactive tasks in the Exam expert section.
5. Prepare 6 subject areas for the Conversation phase from either List A or List B.

3 Complete the quiz on the Grade 10 exam and then compare your answers with your partner before checking with your teacher.

25m
notes on
topic prep
1. How long is the whole exam?
2. What do you have to give to the examiner at the beginning of the examination?

discursive
3. What kind of presentation should you prepare?

5 Min
4. How long is your presentation?

keep conv going
5. What responsibilities have you got during the Interactive phase?

3
6. How many listening texts are there in the Listening phase?

6
7. How many subject areas do you need to prepare for the Conversation phase?

1 - teens
2 - more
Mature/
adult
8. What is the difference between List A and List B?

4 Write the name of the subject area that each question (1-8) is relevant to.

List A

School
Curriculum
1. Are there any school subjects which you would consider redundant and if so, why?

communication
Internet
2. In your view, have we become too dependent on the Internet?

signer
goods
3. Is the purchase of designer goods just a way of showing off to your friends?

communication
4. Do you find it easier to express yourself on the telephone or in an email?

Units 10-12 Self-evaluation

Write Y (yes) or N (needs more practice) for the following statements.

1. ☐ I can talk about designer goods and/or the future of the planet.

2. ☐ I can talk about communication and/or social issues.

3. ☐ I can talk about youth behaviour and/or international events.

4. ☐ I can use more advanced forms of the passive.

5. ☐ I can use modifiers and collocations.

Now you write 'can do' statements like the ones above for the interactive and communicative skills you have practised in Units 10-12.

Beginning of Exam

You will go into the examination room and exchange greetings.

> **Examiner**: Hello. My name's Tricia. What's your name?
>
> **Candidate**: My name's Maria Casali.
>
> **Examiner**: That's Maria Casali, Grade 9?
>
> **Candidate**: Yes.
>
> **Examiner**: Nice to meet you, Maria. Can I check your identification, please?

1 Focus on the Topic presentation

It is very important that you choose a topic that you are interested in, are prepared to research and that will include the language required for the grade. It should not be taken from one of the subject areas. It is advisable to prepare brief notes or a diagram, but this should not be a written script or be memorised. At Grade 10 you are expected to produce a handout to give to the examiner. The Grade 10 topic is a formal discursive presentation and the examiner will take notes to use during the discussion.

Ideas for topics

What is friendship?	The development of rock music in the '60s
My favourite novel	Changing cities in the twenty-first century
The history of dance	My research into child psychology
Football violence	The election of Obama

2 Focus on the Topic discussion

The examiner will be interested in asking you for more information about your topic, as well as finding out about your opinions and developing a discussion between you both. While you are preparing your topic, try and think about the questions the examiner might ask you. You also need to actively engage the examiner in the discussion of your topic so prepare your own questions and comments. Make every effort to use the functions and grammar of the grade in the topic phase and discussion.

Grade 9

> **Examiner**: We'll start with the topic. So, we are going to talk about...
>
> **Candidate**: Today I'd like to talk about the development of rock music in the '60s.

> **Examiner**: Do you feel that today's musicians have been influenced by bands like the Beatles and the Rolling Stones?
>
> **Candidate**: Oh yes, without a doubt. I think most of the recent bands listen to '60s music a great deal and you can see this in their music.

> **Examiner**: Which of these phones would you like to buy?
>
> **Candidate**: Well, if I could afford it, I'd buy a touch screen phone. They are absolutely amazing!

> **Examiner**: What should you have done to get into university?
>
> **Candidate**: Well, let me think. I suppose, I should certainly have worked harder.

Grade 10

Examiner: Now let's begin with your presentation. What is the title and do you have any notes to give me?

Candidate: Yes, certainly. I would like to talk about Shakespeare, his life and work. Here is a copy of my notes.

Candidate: I may be wrong of course, but it seems to me the media takes far too much interest in the private lives of celebrities Don't you agree?

Examiner: Oh yes. I think you're absolutely right!

Candidate: That's the end of my presentation about youth unemployment in my country. Would you like to ask me any questions?

Examiner: Thank you very much. Yes, now you said that unemployment is worse among graduates. What do you think are the reasons for this?

3 Focus on the Interactive phase

In the Interactive phase the examiner will describe a situation to you and you will have to ask questions to find out more, comment and express opinions. It is very important that you keep the conversation going and involve the examiner in the interaction. If you don't maintain the interaction then the phase may end early which may affect your mark. You should use the functions of the grade which should arise naturally from the prompt. At Grade 10, in addition to expressing language functions, you should also show your ability to control the grammar listed for the grade and previous grades.

Grade 9

At the beginning of the Interactive phase the examiner will say to you:

'For the next part, I'll tell you something. Then you have to ask me questions to find out more information and make comments. You need to keep the conversation going. After about four minutes, I'll end the conversation. Are you ready?'

Grade 10

At the beginning of the Interactive phase the examiner will say to you:

'In this task, I'll start by telling you something. You'll have to ask me questions to find out more information and make comments. It's your responsibility to maintain the conversation. Are you ready?'

You may ask the examiner to repeat the prompt if necessary.

Prompt 1

Examiner: My boyfriend really adores climbing. Recently he persuaded me to go on a climbing holiday with him in the Alps. It was a terrible mistake.

Candidate: Really! Why was it such a terrible mistake?

Examiner: Well, the worst thing was I was absolutely terrified.

Candidate: That must have been awful. Didn't your boyfriend help you?

Prompt 2

Examiner: Young people do seem to be rather unhealthy these days. I think I know the reason for this.

Candidate: What do you think the reason is?

Examiner: Well, of course the main reason is the fact they eat so much fast food.

Candidate: Do they? I don't think they do much in my country, apart from perhaps pizza. What kind of fast food do you mean?

Here are some more examples of prompts which you might hear in the Interactive phase of Grade 9 and Grade 10. Practise responding to these prompts with a partner.

Grade 9

1. I really would like to get a job abroad but I've got friends and family here, so I'm not sure if it's the right decision.

2. I went on holiday to India for 2 weeks last year but it really wasn't long enough to see the whole country and get to know the people. Perhaps I should have gone for longer.

3. When I went to university my outlook on life changed totally and it wasn't just the studying.

4. My son left school when he was very young and I think he will live to regret it. So many missed opportunities.

5. My best friend has 5 children and absolutely adores them. The only problem is that she is very protective of them and doesn't give them any freedom. I don't think she is giving them the opportunity to grow up and mature.

6. You won't believe what happened to my sister. Well she's always loved singing and entered one of these TV talent competitions. I never thought she was that good but she actually won!

7. My father always used to talk to me about the importance of education, but he really meant school and university. I think education is broader than that.

8. Of course I hope my children will be happy in the future, but there are three things that I would particularly like to happen to them.

Grade 10

1. I have always been a vegetarian, but sometimes I have a problem explaining to my friends the reasons why.

2. There was an interesting article in the paper the other day explaining why there is a high rate of unemployment among young people these days.

3. My best friend can be really annoying. She's really nice but often doesn't tell me the truth, and this makes me rather suspicious of her.

4. Sometimes I think children spend far too much time on the computer. They never seem to spend any time playing sports or even actually talking to their friends.

5. In my view, it's high time everybody took some responsibility for saving the planet. There are so many things we could all do.

6. Sometimes when I read the newspapers I wonder how much of what I read is true. It seems to me every story is exaggerated and sensationalised.

4 Focus on Listening (ONLY Grade 10)

After you have finished the Interactive phase, you will move on to the Listening, the fourth phase of the Grade 10 exam. You will listen to three short listening texts, two of Type 1 and one of Type 2.

The listening texts are not related to any of the given subject areas for conversation. They may refer to everyday situations, the work place or unexpected events. Your answer will only be a few words and you will not need to take notes. You will only hear each listening text once.

The examiner will say to you:

'I'm going to read you three short passages and after I've finished each one, I'd like you to either suggest a suitable ending or answer a question. I'll then move on to the next passage. Are you ready?'

Type 1 Listening task

For Type 1 Listening task you will be asked to provide a suitable ending to the passage and the examiner will usually finish speaking in the middle of a sentence which you are expected to complete. Although the texts are quite short, you will need a high level of listening skills to be able to make predictions or deductions or to understand what is being inferred. You will need to make decisions about context, people and the narrative using your knowledge of grammar, vocabulary and language style to do this. You should only say a few words to complete the last sentence so if you say a few sentences, you have probably misunderstood the text. Sometimes there are several possible answers but they will be very similar.

Before you start the Type 1 tasks, the examiner will say:

'These two passages are incomplete. When I stop, I'd like you to tell me in just a few words how you think the passage finishes.'

When the examiner stops speaking you will complete the sentence and then the examiner will move on to the second passage.

Type 2 Listening task

For Type 2 Listening the examiner will read a listening text and then ask you to answer a question about such things as the context or the people involved. You need to use your knowledge of grammar, vocabulary and language style to identify what exactly the passage is describing or what place, job or activity is being referred to. Your answer should be no more than a few words. You should take care to listen to the entire passage so that you can answer the examiner's question accurately.

Before you start the Type 2 Listening task the examiner will say:

'After I've read this passage, I'll ask you about what you've heard.'

Sample Listening tasks Type 1

Here are some examples of Type 1 Listening tasks which you might hear in the Grade 10 Listening phase.

The answers are on page 95.

Example

The wedding sounded as if it was going to be absolutely perfect. A beautiful setting in a little country church with stunning bouquets of flowers everywhere. Hundreds of us were waiting in the church and the magnificent wedding march started up. We looked around, the bridegroom paced up and down anxiously but there was still no sign...

Possible answer: *of the bride*

1   I have always been a committed vegetarian and although I occasionally eat fish, I never eat meat. Well, on Saturday I went to a restaurant with friends and ordered the special vegetarian meal. I was just staring my meal when I looked down and saw in front of me large chunks...

2   Jane was delighted to be pregnant and was telling everyone how excited she was, but she knew there was one thing she had to do and she had to do it immediately. She would have liked to have had one more but reluctantly threw away her last packet because now she really did have to give up...

3   The film had had brilliant reviews. Apparently the acting and direction were superb and the plot very exciting. Imagine our disappointment then when we sat through the 3-hour film and were totally...

4   John fell madly in love with Jane. She was beautiful, intelligent and had a great sense of humour. He then proposed to her within a week despite the fact they hardly knew each other. I think he's completely...

5   I woke up in a complete panic. I had overslept and my flight was taking off in 1 hour. I hastily threw my stuff into a bag and jumped into a taxi. The taxi driver raced through the heavy traffic and dropped me off outside the airport terminal. I looked up at the departure board and was dismayed to see my flight to New York...

6   My husband and I always agree about everything. We love going to the same concerts, agree on the latest novels and usually want to see the same kind of films. Sometimes we even choose the same dish on the menu when we go out for a meal. Imagine my surprise at the last general election when I found out we were voting...

7   I keep on trying to get my family to separate glass, cans and newspapers but they never listen to me and just throw everything in the same bin. I've explained numerous times how important it is to protect the environment but I just can't persuade them to...

Sample Listening tasks Type 2

Here are some examples of Type 2 Listening tasks which you might hear in the Grade 10 Listening phase. The answers are on page 95.

Example

It's just ridiculous! Night after night of beautiful young people singing or dancing and then you have the nasty comments and the tears. I suppose it's good for the successful contestants who perhaps have a really good chance of becoming rich and famous.

Question: *What is the speaker describing?* **Answer**: *A talent show*

---

1 I go to the market really early and try to buy the freshest and most beautiful ones available. Nowadays they come from all over the world. In fact, what I enjoy the most is preparing for special occasions like weddings and parties. I am quite artistic and like creating unusual designs with subtle and unusual colours.

Question: What is the speaker's job?

2 I work in a big city so it can be quite a dangerous job especially with the rise in violent crime these days. Most of the time I'm out on the beat making sure the community stays safe and I find this very satisfying. I'm not very keen on all the paperwork, though. I'd rather be working with people than pen pushing.

Question: What is the speaker's job?

3 It's absolutely freezing and everybody is shivering and wrapped up warm in woolly hats and thick jackets. The sky is icy grey and suddenly as you look up tiny white fluffy balls come fluttering down on people's heads or drop lightly down on the ground. Laughter and excitement abound as winter has finally arrived.

Question: What is the speaker talking about?

4 Ok everyone, you're doing a great job but you need to start working together better. Strikers, don't be greedy - you need to start passing the ball more. Remember what we have been doing in training, ok?

Question: Who is speaking?

5 I love my job, but it can be very demanding. I work long hours and do lots of preparation and essay marking. But there is quite a lot of job satisfaction when I see them graduate.

Question: Where does the speaker work?

6 It's very exhilarating and I enjoy it, but you do have to know what you are doing, understand currents and be confident in the water. Learning to stand is the hardest part! It's not much fun when you fall in!

Question: What activity is the speaker describing?

7 A recent US survey showed that only 38% of Americans worry about global warming. The majority of respondents believed climate change wouldn't not harm them personally, and that it is more of a worry for future generations.

Question: How do Americans feel about the effects of global warming?

8 Are you fed-up with working the usual 9-5? Bored with British weather? Need a change of scenery? Well, come and work in the sunshine all year round and experience different cultures everyday! Call TopMed Cruises today to learn what exciting opportunities await you!

Question: What is the speaker's purpose?

5 Focus on the Conversation

The examiner will ask you about two of the listed subject areas for the grade. You will have prepared all these subjects and will be familiar with vocabulary and discussion areas. At Grade 10 you will already have chosen from either List A (for younger/less mature candidates) or List B. You should contribute opinions and ideas and demonstrate your knowledge of the language of the grade by using the functions and grammar specified in the syllabus. You should share responsibility with the examiner for the direction and maintenance of the conversation.

Grade 9

Examiner: Let's move on to the Conversation phase. Let's talk about crime and punishment. Do you think prison is always the best form of punishment for criminals?
Candidate: Well, in my view, it depends on the kind of crime they have committed.

Examiner : What do you think is the most important technological invention in recent years?
Candidate : Oh, certainly the computer. Don't you agree?

Examiner : If you could choose, what kind of design would you like for your new home?
Candidate : Personally, I prefer traditional rather than contemporary. I live in quite an old house with very interesting architecture.

Examiner : Let's talk about global environmental issues. What do you think we should have done in the past to prevent environmental disasters such as the oil spill in the Gulf of Mexico. '
Candidate : In that particular case I think they should have taken more safety precautions. You know, these big companies just want to make more money but we ought to have found a more environmentally-friendly source of energy a long time ago. Don't you agree?

Examiner : I didn't quite catch that. Do you mean that dreams and nightmares really relate to personal events in our lives?
Candidate : Oh, absolutely. I can give you many examples of dreams that I have had that seem to accurately predict what happens to me later on.

Grade 10

Examiner : Let's turn to roles in the family. Do you think traditional family roles have changed in your country in recent years?
Candidate : Yes, indeed. For example, my father now helps in the house and often cooks in the evening. My mother has a demanding job and often doesn't get home till late.

Examiner : Do you think people spend too much money on designer goods?
Candidate : Absolutely! I think it is quite immoral to spend that much money on a watch or handbag.

Examiner : I'd like us to talk about international events. How far do you think international events bring the world closer together?
Candidate : In many cases I don't think they do at all, especially political meetings for world leaders. Ordinary people just don't feel involved, do they? But I do think music festivals, things like that can bring people around the world together, give them a greater understanding of other cultures and so on.

Examiner : Let's talk about stress management. Stress seems to be quite a problem these days. What do you think are the reasons for this?
Candidate : Firstly, I think people have very busy lives and probably take on too much. Then there is so much pressure to be successful and have a good lifestyle. It can be very difficult, can't it?

Pairwork material

Unit 1, page 7, exercise 2b

These scores show how much each of your answers is worth. Add up your total score and find out how techy you are.

1 A3; B1; C1
2 A2; B3; C1
3 A3; B2; C1
4 A2; B1; C3

5 A2; B3; C1
6 A3; B1; C3
7 A2; B3; C1
8 A1; B2; C3

- If you scored 20 to 24 you are very techy.
- If you scored 12 and 19 you are getting there.
- If you scored 11 or less you are living with the dinosaurs!

Unit 2, page 11, exercise 10c

Look at the following statements about the Interactive phase and decide whether they are true (T), false (F) or don't know (DK).

1 ☐ You take control.
2 ☐ You don't ask any questions.
3 ☐ The emphasis is on your grammar.
4 ☐ You can tell lies.
5 ☐ You should use the functions of the grade.
6 ☐ You should start the conversation.
7 ☐ You should stop talking if you haven't got anything else to say.
8 ☐ The phase may last 9 minutes.

Unit 5, page 35, exercise d

1 Where do you wish you lived?
2 What do you love doing?
3 What do you hope to do in the future?
4 What should you have done to prepare for this exam?

Unit 6, page 43, exercise 12b

Student A

1 I r___ ___k I've made some terrible decisions in the past. I just hope I don't make the ___ ___e mistakes in th___ ___.
2 I ___ ___eed to make a dramatic change in my lifestyle but I'm not sure where to start.

Unit 7, page 51, exercise 12b

1 Expected response: *She had got a new job.*
2 Expected response: *The sun came out.*

12c
Expected response: a music festival / rock concert.

Appendix 1   Pairwork material

Unit 6, page 43, exercise 12b

Student B

1   My husband and I saw something very strange going on at our neighbour's house last night and we don't know whether to keep quiet about it or not.

2   If I'd taken that job in New York, my life would have been quite different.

Unit 9, page 58, exercise 1a

Compulsory School subjects in England

Art & Design

Design & Technology

Geography

Information, Communication & Technology (ICT)

Modern Foreign languages

Physical Education

Science

Citizenship

English

History

Mathematics

Music

Religious Education

Unit 9, page 62, exercise 8b

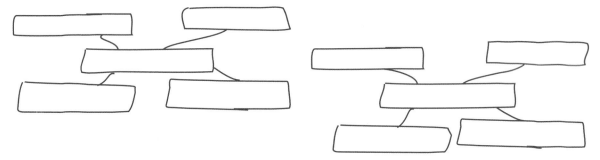

Unit 12, page 81, exercise 8a

Student B

Give one point for every sentence (1-5) with which you agree and deduct one point from every sentence (A-E) with which you agree. How many points did you give?

Score card B

1   ☐ He/she enjoyed the presentation.

2   ☐ He/she spoke for five minutes.

3   ☐ He/she sometimes looked at me.

4   ☐ The presentation had a clear structure.

5   ☐ He/she gave me some helpful notes.

A   ☐ He/she memorised the presentation.

B   ☐ He/she spoke for too long and I had to interrupt.

C   ☐ He/she spoke too quickly.

D   ☐ He/she looked bored.

E   ☐ I wasn't given any notes.

Trinity Takeaway, page 90

Listening task Type 1 answers

1   of meat
2   smoking
3   bored/unimpressed
4   mad

5   had already left/was boarding
6   for different parties
7   recycle

Trinity Takeaway, page 91

Listening task Type 2 answers

1   a florist/works in a flower shop
2   a policeman
3   the first snow/snowing
4   a football coach

5   university
6   surfing/windsurfing
7   They don't think they will affect them personally
8   to advertise jobs on a cruise ship